WHAT'S THE BIG IDEA?

WHAT'S THE BIG IDEA?

CREATING AND CAPITALIZING ON THE BEST MANAGEMENT THINKING

THOMAS H. DAVENPORT
LAURENCE PRUSAK

WITH H. JAMES WILSON

HARVARD BUSINESS SCHOOL PRESS

BOSTON, MASSACHUSETTS

Library of Congress Cataloging-in-Publication Data
Davenport, Thomas H.
    What's the big idea? : creating and capitalizing on the best management
thinking / Thomas H. Davenport Laurence Prusak with H. James Wilson.
        p. cm.
    ISBN 1-57851-931-4 (alk. paper)
    1. Creative ability in business. 2. Knowledge management. 3. Success
in business. I. Prusak, Laurence. II. Wilson, H. James. III. Title.
    HD53.D38 2003
    658--dc21

                                                          2002155934

The paper used in this publication meets the requirements of the American National Standard for Permanence of Paper for Publications and Documents in Libraries and Archives Z39.48-1992.

CONTENTS

PREFACE

THE AUTHORS of this book have spent our work lives immersed in business ideas. First at school and then professionally, we've never really been anything but writers, researchers, consultants, and teachers, and we have only had "real jobs" for brief periods. In fact, we have together worked more than fifty years for a combination of eight consulting firms, ten universities, and various other educational or research-oriented institutions. We point this out not so much to boast—in fact it suggests that we have a hard time holding down a job—but to better account for the often overlooked link between personal experience and objective insight. After fifty years of thinking about and working with business ideas and the "gurus" who create them, it finally occurred to us that they were important enough to deserve a book of their own!

However, as we thought more about the topic and conducted research on it, our primary focus began to shift. For a couple of decades, whenever we had researched and consulted on business ideas, we'd worked inside organizations with people who made it their business to bring in the ideas, modify them to suit their organizations, and shepherd them to implementation. During the lives of these research initiatives, we noticed that quite a few of the same people were joining us, even as our program themes changed from information technology management to reengineering to information management to knowledge management. Some stayed with us even when they switched from one firm or one industry to another. We are well aware it wasn't our personal charm or charisma that attracted these individuals to what could be a time-consuming and somewhat expensive endeavor. We began to realize that these practitioners were, more or less, intrinsically motivated. What they wanted to do, what they felt they *should* do, was assess and translate and develop new ideas to bring into their organizations and subsequently fight for them. And quite a fight it often was, especially if the ideas were innovative or could threaten the status quo.

We'd thought of these people as collaborators, clients, and friends, but had never really focused on their roles and their importance to the world of business and management ideas. In this book we call them *idea practitioners*. Like Molière's Monsieur Jourdain, who had been speaking prose for years without knowing it, we've been working closely with idea practitioners without ever labeling them as such or even being conscious of their considerable importance to our own success.

One reason for our lack of awareness is that few people recognize that idea practitioners actually *have* a "practice" within organizations. That is, these idea practitioners possess common goals, tactics, vocabularies, methods of working, stories, myths, legends, and all the overt and covert activities that make up a practice. One can think of law, medicine, and even consulting as a practice. Of course, there is great regional and even organizational variety within practices as within most collective activities. However, there remains a core set of recognizable activities that would enable one practitioner to spot another one in action across a country or a continent.

Giving recognition to idea practitioners was one of the spurs to writing this book. Although their work is the primary story, another group of people also plays a significant role in idea-driven business change: the active management writers and theorists whom we and others call gurus. Ranging from Nobel laureates to semireputable popularizers, these people undertake varied forms and types of research and then broadcast their news. They form a key component of the larger advice industry that has grown enormously since the 1980s, and that has subsequently increased the gurus' renown and compensation. It would be far more difficult for our friends the practitioners to enact their practice without the rhetoric, structure, and legitimization that our guru friends offer. Although gurus are a well-known commodity in the business world, their work is sometimes disparaged as faddish. We wanted to shed a more positive—or at least an objective—light on the gurus and their ideas.

We dedicate this book to the idea practitioners, and tip our hats to the gurus. The two groups form an ecology of ideas, with its own dynamics, that has powerful effects, for both good and occasionally ill, within most large organizations in the world today.

We'd also like to acknowledge the contributions of some thinkers we know—and some we don't. The most important in the latter category is Richard Posner, who wrote a book called *Public Intellectuals*.[1] Posner's book was controversial and, possibly, politically biased, but one of his main points was surely correct: People who pursue, develop, and produce ideas for the public have a far greater influence on public life than is often understood. We would agree, adding that our own collection of what could be called public business intellectuals has an even greater influence on most people's day-to-day lives than Posner's group has. Public business intellectuals have the same role, in a sense, that Shelley attributed to poets: They are the "unacknowledged legislators of mankind."

In addition to Posner, we had substantial help from two anonymous people who reviewed our book for Harvard Business

School Press. The best reviewer, however, revealed his identity to us, and we therefore thank Bob Sutton for his very insightful comments. Bob is a guru himself (number fifty-nine on our list of gurus) and has plenty of more lucrative things to do with his time than reading and commenting on our book. We'd say the same about other gurus who were generous with their time: Warren Bennis, Jim Collins, Fred Reichheld, and Tom Stewart were our guru interviewees. We're also very grateful to all the idea practitioners—identified in appendix B—who allowed us to interview them and confirmed or edited their remarks. Art Henderson, another idea practitioner, gave us a thorough reading and detailed comments.

A number of colleagues assisted with this book. Margaret Stergios tirelessly searched, calculated, and recalculated the guru rankings as we identified new names as candidates. Don Cohen gave us a careful reading of the manuscript at an early stage. Winnie Wong and Alyssa Bottone helped us manage our relationships with the idea practitioner interviewees. Alex Beal helped us with marketing the book and the ideas. Mike May sponsored the project at the Accenture Institute for Strategic Change and helped connect us with the rest of the firm.

Melinda Merino was an effective and caring editor who at least appeared to find this project fascinating and made helpful suggestions all along the way. We're sure there are a lot of other people at HBS Press whom we should thank, but Melinda insulated us from any complexity in that highly capable organization's processes.

Our families supplied the usual level of authorial support, and perhaps a bit more. Ben and Kim Prusak transcribed many of our recorded interviews. Jodi Davenport, Brenda Prusak, and Susan Wilson read and commented on the manuscript. Hayes and Chase Davenport and Ben and Brooke Wilson were just great kids, and that was plenty.

In any case, here is our take on what idea practitioners are up to, how they and their organizations turn ideas into reality, and how those who aspire to the practice of business ideas can become more effective. This book is offered in the spirit of admiration for this necessary but poorly rewarded and little-understood activity. However, the light of passion and satisfaction in the eyes of those who love ideas and love seeing them put to work appears to be compensation enough.

WHAT'S THE BIG IDEA?

1

WINNING WITH IDEAS

HOW BUSINESS IDEAS ARE LINKED
TO BUSINESS SUCCESS

Westinghouse corporation was an innovative firm—at least in terms of the products and services it offered to the marketplace. The company brought to market the electric power plant, air brakes, the shock absorber, nuclear power, commercial radio, radar, frost-free refrigerators, and many other, less dramatic innovations. Yet despite its product discoveries, Westinghouse is effectively dead as a company, its businesses dismantled and sold off. Its death came as no surprise, as its financial performance had languished for many years.

As an interesting comparison, General Electric, Westinghouse's competitor since the late nineteenth century, is currently the world's most valuable corporation. Since the 1980s, the company delivered more than 20 percent annual growth to shareholders each year. GE's recently retired CEO, Jack Welch, is lionized as a management genius (though the revelation of his excessive retirement perks hasn't helped this aura), and his autobiography sat atop best-seller lists. *Fortune* magazine named Welch manager of the century. The same magazine named GE the most admired ιny in America three years in a row, and the *Financial Times* did the same for three years with the Most Admired Company in the World award. Like Westinghouse, GE became a diverse conglomerate, and several of its businesses overlapped with Westinghouse's: broadcasting, power generation, industrial equipment, financing, and so on. Why did GE rise to the top of the industrial heap, whereas its once-powerful rival sank into the graveyard? Why did GE's financial performance shoot off the charts, whereas Westinghouse's descended into oblivion?

Many factors can explain the disparity in these companies' fortunes, but one factor is surely their different embrace of ideas for business improvement. Westinghouse had innovative products, but the only business notions it pursued involved financial analysis, acquisition and (more often) divestiture, and a late-in-the-game approach to quality. GE, particularly under Welch but before him as well, was a hotbed of managerial innovations. Though known as an innovative company, GE has that reputation primarily for its innovative business and management ideas, rather than for any breakthrough products or services. In their time, earlier CEOs, such as Ralph Cordiner and Reg Jones, were just as celebrated as Welch for embracing innovative business ideas.

From the beginning, Westinghouse was run by scientists and engineers who had little interest in business innovation. George Westinghouse himself founded 60 companies, and the various businesses (eventually 172) within the conglomerate were generally left to manage themselves if their individual financial results were satisfactory. By the early 1980s, financial results had become the overriding focus of corporate headquarters. Shareholder value was the only consideration; everything else was expendable.

Virtually the only managerial innovation ever recorded at Westinghouse was a financial planning tool called Vabastram (for value-based strategic management). Vabastram used quantitative analysis to assess whether a business unit should be kept or sold. The tool justified a few acquisitions and many divestitures. The several CEOs of Westinghouse in the latter half of the twentieth century had almost exclusively financial goals (raising return on equity and stock price) and took financial actions (stock buy-backs, manipulating profits, and selling assets). Over the company's last fourteen years (from 1983 to 1997), Westinghouse's stock price rose 126 percent (three-quarters of the rise coming when it announced it was getting out of all industrial businesses). Over the same period, GE's stock rose 931 percent.

When Michael Jordan (not the basketball player, but the former CEO of Frito-Lay) arrived as Westinghouse's first outsider CEO in 1993, a newspaper reporter notes that he was most bothered by the company's insular culture: "There was little exchanging of ideas among upper managers, the sort of water cooler bull sessions about strategy, new businesses or new ways of doing things. This is what had become familiar to him during his years as a consultant and PepsiCo executive. But these guys at Westinghouse were engineers, not entrepreneurs."[1]

At GE, on the other hand, new business ideas were avidly pursued and viewed as part of the company's fabric. Certainly, the company sought financial targets, bought and sold many businesses, and made much of its money in the late 1990s from its GE Capital subsidiary. But at the same time that Westinghouse was slowly declining, GE was successfully implementing ideas. In the 1950s, CEO Cordiner spoke of "customer focus" and "decentralization as a management philosophy" to empower each GE employee to "bring out his full resources and enthusiastic cooperation." Cordiner sponsored a formal planning program, but unlike Vabastram at Westinghouse, it focused on "continuous innovation in products, processes, facilities, methods, organization, leadership, and all other aspects of the business."[2]

GE under Welch in the 1980s and 1990s was a veritable idea (and profit) machine. Although GE certainly remained a conglomerate under his leadership, he banned the term and focused on the integration of related businesses. He trumpeted the concepts of Work-Out; "boundarylessness"; speed, simplicity, and self-confidence; Six Sigma; and digitization, among several other ideas. His letter in GE's annual report became a reliable place to find the management ideas that would reshape GE—and many other firms—over the subsequent months and years.

Welch and GE didn't just talk about ideas; they embraced them with a bear hug. This approach continues today. Once an idea becomes a corporate initiative, it gets embedded into the company's so-called Operating System, or way of managing itself. The four key initiatives of the early twenty-first century—globalization, Six Sigma, growing services businesses, and digitization— are discussed and monitored in at least one management meeting each month of the year. The Operating System is described by GE as follows: "It is a year-round series of intense learning sessions in which business CEOs, role models, and initiative champions from GE as well as outside companies, meet and share the intellectual capital of the world: its best ideas."[3]

GE also sticks with its ideas and doesn't treat them as fads. Globalization has been through more than a dozen annual cycles. Six Sigma has gone through five, services orientation six, and e-business three.[4]

As a highly visible CEO, Welch got a lot of credit for using management ideas to revitalize GE. But he doesn't deserve all the credit. Welch surrounded himself with an informal network of advisers, including academics, consultants, and GE employees. We'll label all the internal advisers *idea practitioners*. The company's education center at Crotonville, New York, became "idea central," or the nexus of all these idea-oriented people. It became a place to bring in ideas from external academics and gurus, to refine the ideas to make them fit GE, and to train GE managers to apply the ideas themselves. Welch himself showed up at the center twice a month; the revitalization of Crotonville was one of his first acts as CEO.[5] His commitment of time was a strong, tangible message that ideas counted at GE.

The GE idea practitioners were world-class. Welch first hired Noel Tichy, a well-known University of Michigan business school professor, to run Crotonville and the related idea processes at GE

for a couple of years while Tichy was on leave from the university.[6] Later, Jim Baughman, a Harvard Business School professor,
took over the center. Among other ideas, Baughman introduced
the famous Work-Out program, which combines process improvement and employee morale-building.[7] The raw idea came
from discussions with workers at GE's Louisville, Kentucky, ap-
pliance factory. Afterward, Baughman and Welch refined the concept and tried it at Crotonville sessions, where it was enormously
successful. An account of the creation of the idea illustrates
Welch's appetite for ideas at GE:

> To translate the idea of Work-Out into reality, Baughman called
> a meeting of the Crotonville faculty, many of whom were profes-
> sors or consultants, in September 1988. With 30 management
> thinkers in the room, Welch presented his view of what he called
> the "GE Engine"—a corporation fueled by financial, strategic,
> and organizational success. He maintained that the company
> had made good progress in the financial and strategic areas, but
> had a long way to go in the organizational area. . . . Following
> this presentation, the faculty debated with Welch how to make
> his ideas happen. . . . Following the Crotonville meeting, Welch
> and Baughman continued to talk about the idea of Work-Out.
> Eventually, the rough sketch of a process began to emerge.[8]

In 1994 Welch hired a former business school dean and prominent management thinker, Steve Kerr, to run Crotonville. Kerr
had held numerous influential positions (see chapter 9). He had
been a highly respected professor and consultant in the fields of
organizational behavior and motivation, the dean of faculty at
the University of Southern California's business school, a faculty
member at Crotonville, and a consultant to GE on the Work-Out
process. Collaborating with Welch, Kerr further refined the Work-
Out process and evangelized for the notion of boundarylessness—
that good ideas should be able to cross any boundary within GE
and outside the company as well.[9] Welch was so proud of the role
of Crotonville and the ideas and idea practitioners rooted there

that when he retired, the facility was renamed the John F. Welch Leadership Center.

Of course, other factors besides ideas and idea practitioners account for GE's success and Westinghouse's demise. Furthermore, GE is hardly the perfect organization. But there's no denying that GE's managerial culture was more dynamic and vibrant than Westinghouse's at a time when investment analysts began to study companies closely. And the most financially oriented analyst would admit that the perceived managerial vitality of a company is an important factor in its stock price. It's difficult to prove definitively that GE was a more idea-driven and better-managed company than Westinghouse, but GE certainly managed to create that impression—and to create substantially better long-term results.

Ideas and Idea Practitioners in Business

This book is for people who believe, or at least are willing to be persuaded, that new ideas are vitally important to businesses. It's for managers and other professionals who care not only about the bottom line of financial outcomes, but also about how the organization achieves its results. Businesspeople who want to be personally involved in putting forward ideas in business, either to advance their own careers or to benefit their organizations, will benefit from this book. So will passionate individuals who want to lead with ideas. As at GE, we call all these people idea practitioners, and how they work and succeed is at the core of this book.

By *ideas,* we mean approaches to improving business performance and management. Our primary concern in this book is not ideas for new products or services that companies can take to the marketplace. Although an important topic, it is already the focus of many books. We are talking instead about ideas that will rev up internal performance; ideas like total quality management, reengineering, knowledge management, activity-based costing, worker empowerment, balanced scorecards, and a thousand other notions with the potential to get a business in better shape. (See appendix A for a more complete list.) Of course, some business improvement ideas can be taken to the market by companies selling services, software, or even tangible goods like office equipment. For example, a communication equipment company might sell not only telephones and switches, but also ideas about how to improve communications within and across organizations. Companies that sell idea-oriented products and services should be particularly focused on idea practitioners, because they are their primary customers and influencers for other buyers.

For managers and professionals already convinced of the importance of business ideas and of the value of a career as an idea practitioner, this book is intended to serve another function. It provides a set of tools and frameworks to help idea practitioners do their jobs. How do you decide which ideas are the most worthy of your time and attention? How can you avoid fads and bring about true change? How can others be enlisted in idea-focused initiatives? We aim to provide ways to generate these insights and more.

The Functions of Business and Management Ideas

When well executed, new business ideas help organizations in several ways. Like any other form of rhetoric, ideas can inspire, motivate, and bring energy to both individuals and organizations; people are encouraged to work harder and try again. New business ideas can also lead to increased organizational vitality and renewal. They serve as motivation for organizational change, which helps an organization adapt to its environment. Many business ideas also involve a self-assessment step, in which an organization can benefit from looking at and listening to itself and how it does its work. New business ideas can energize individuals, leading them to work harder and to think more creatively. Doing the same job over and over again each day—no matter how initially interesting it may have been—can become very boring unless there are new ideas blowing through often.

Although new business ideas do not always improve business performance, they often do. For example, a company successfully employs quality management, reengineering, strategic planning, or knowledge management, and its performance improves measurably. GE got great results with its Work-Out program, including 80 percent reductions in the cycle time for milling steel in Schenectady, New York, and $200 million inventory reductions in its appliance business in Louisville.[10] Taco Bell dramatically upgraded growth and per-store revenues through reengineering. BP increased the oil exploration hit rate and reduced equipment downtime through knowledge management. We could go on for many pages—as we and others have in other books—with examples and case studies.

However, there is no empirical evidence that simply adopting new business ideas leads to stronger business performance. In fact, a study by Barry Staw at the University of California, Berkeley, suggests that there is no *overall* relationship between ideas and performance.[11] We'd argue that some organizations do a good job of implementing programs based on new ideas, and some do it badly. Therefore, it's unlikely that any overall correlation with performance would be found across multiple firms.

Some companies manage to use new ideas to consistently improve performance—just as they employ other managerial resources to be successful. One such company is Dell Computer, a leading company of the 1990s and one of the few information technology firms that has prospered even during the hard times of the early twenty-first century. Dell has a strong proclivity to use new business ideas for one purpose: to improve its performance. John Egan, director of manufacturing for Dell's desktops and enterprise systems, specializes in bringing in—or motivating others to bring in—new manufacturing and supply chain ideas at Dell. These ideas impact the customer experience by providing custom-configured systems in the most efficient and direct manner. At this relentless firm, ambitious goal-setting drives managers to seek better ideas both inside and outside the company. During an interview, Egan described Dell's receptivity to new ideas:

> *We were building a new facility to manufacture desktops, where you have to improve dramatically in a competitive market. So, we challenged the team planning the move to double the people and space productivity of the current operations. This drove them to look for innovative approaches and new technologies to meet the goals. We introduced a "change the game" strategy that included going vertical to utilize space, eliminated the need for a warehouse, removed touches and time for 100% "lot size one" custom configuration, and integrated new supply chain software utilizing our consulting partners. We encouraged engineers and production associates to come up with new ideas, and we funded pilots. Pretty quickly we were producing about six times more in terms of units per hour. We say that "Dell's Law" is to do it faster, better and with less inventory while enhancing the customer experience.*

Of course, companies that don't see new business ideas as driving performance as Dell does will lower the average correlation between those two variables.

Even for all companies combined, however, the Staw study suggests that there is a relationship between adopting new business ideas and *perceived* business performance. Companies that embrace new ideas are likely to have higher stock prices and to appear on "most admired" lists. Both investment analysts and the press seem to believe that companies that adopt new ideas are better companies than those that do not. One study of investment analysts suggested that 35 percent of their investment decisions are based on nonfinancial factors, including strategy execution and the quality of strategy, management credibility, innovativeness, and the ability to attract talented people.[12] Each of these nonfinancial factors can be strongly affected by how organizations deal with new management ideas.

John Egan, Idea Practitioner

John Egan, the head of manufacturing for Dell's desktops, servers, and enterprise systems, could be considered a supply-chain idea magnet. Egan worked at IBM in its personal computing business for eighteen years. In 1998, he came to Dell, because he found the direct-to-customer model compelling. He also has been impressed by the continuous process improvement approaches of General Electric. Egan feels that it took him six months to understand the direct model, but after that he began to set goals, encourage innovation, and kick off pilot projects. As Dell's representative to the Leaders for Manufacturing program at the Massachusetts Institute of Technology, he feels that the program turns out a new generation of idea practitioners with each class.

Although we are hard put to quantify precisely the degree to which national economies embrace new business ideas, there clearly are differences. The United States is the world capital of business ideas, with an aggressive idea-creation industry and managers who are enthusiastic about applying business ideas. Hundreds of business magazines and thousands of business books are published every year in the United States. The U.S. economy did very well in the 1980s and 1990s, a period in which it embraced new business ideas with a vengeance. Japan, on the other hand, has not generally been an enthusiastic adopter of new business ideas, except for a strong romance with quality in the manufacturing sector. When Japan was ardently pursuing quality ahead of the rest of the world, its economy thrived. The rest of the world caught up on quality, and Japan's economy has suffered ever since. Although our brief description is no doubt oversimplified, the U.S. manager's love of business ideas is at least partly accountable for the high levels of productivity and growth that the American economy experienced between 1980 and 2000.

Business ideas, then, serve two basic roles for organizations. One is to improve—or try to improve—organizational performance. They don't always work, but new business ideas deliver to organizations improved cost, cycle time, financial performance, market share, and so forth, if implemented well. The other role business ideas play is to provide legitimacy. They indicate that an organization and the individuals within it are diligently attempting to improve their business—whether they truly are or not. In a sort of organizational Hawthorne effect, the rest of the world notices this attempt to improve and is impressed by it.

These two objectives are compatible, as Harvard professor and organizational guru Nitin Nohria has noted.[13] Even when a manager pursues an idea for the legitimacy it provides, he or she will still probably expect some possibility of real benefit. And the more actual performance improvement that organizations receive from a business idea, the more likely the idea is to provide legitimacy. But early adopters of ideas are more likely to be pursuing them for real performance gains, rather than legitimacy. Only after an idea has become popular and widely discussed in the media would it provide much legitimacy. Nohria's research suggests that early adopters of new business ideas (Total Quality Management in his research) take up the ideas when they notice problems in internal operations; later adopters are motivated more by declines in market value and investor ratings—that is, more the external legitimacy of the performance rather than internal performance expectations.

Regardless of whether you believe that pursuing new business ideas is a good approach or a poor one, most individuals have little ability to exclude them from their organizations altogether. The business ideas and advice industry is a large and pervasive one, and unless you work in a very small or remote company, you can count on these ideas playing a role in your organization.

Therefore, it makes sense to try to identify and bring in only the ideas that are of most potential benefit and to make their impact as positive as possible. As they said in some spaceship movie, "Resistance is futile."

Who's Responsible?

Most writers on business ideas place the primary responsibility for the success of the ideas squarely on the shoulders of the business guru. If the idea is successful and becomes pervasive within organizations, it's because the guru is a genius. If the idea is merely a fad, the guru is a goat. The very word *guru* is a somewhat ironic term implying that the individual who holds the title is visionary, mystical, and exotic. There are several tomes devoted to celebrating these people—even some that purport to teach how to become one.[14] Gurus play an important role in the advancement and circulation of business ideas, and we devote a chapter to them in this book. We even rank them so that practicing managers can evaluate the relative standing of the purveyor of their favorite ideas. But the gurus are not the most important factors in the successful use of business ideas.

Instead, our primary focus is on the people within organizations who make ideas a reality. Unlike the gurus, these people have seldom been written about or even identified by other management thinkers, and there's no real name for them. We've labeled them idea practitioners because they put ideas into practice and in turn have developed a practice of idea implementation. As we'll point out later, however, they also help to develop the ideas and in many cases are hybrid creator/practitioners.

These individuals can do both good and harm within their companies. On the negative side, they can implement management ideas in a faddish manner, wasting their organization's time and giving new business ideas a bad name. Chapter 3 explains that there are no totally bad management ideas, only ideas managed badly. Consequently, idea practitioners bear a lot of responsibility for managing ideas well and creating a positive climate for the use of management notions.

But in exchange for all this responsibility, the lion's share of credit belongs to idea practitioners within companies. Ideas are cheap and plentiful, but their implementation is often very difficult. It's these idea practitioners who determine what ideas make sense for their organizations, modify them to suit their needs, and mobilize their organizations to make them real. In many cases, they are idea creators and translators as well as users. They take risks and often use substantial amounts of hard-earned social capital to advance their convictions. We've spent much of the last twenty years of our own work lives in close relationships with these people, and we've come to admire them greatly.

While it's fashionable to attribute all idea-based change within corporations to a visionary CEO, idea practitioners are more likely to be middle managers. Sure, some CEOs have led their organizations to embrace ideas—Jack Welch, John Browne of BP, and John Reed of Citicorp, for example. Gary Loveman, CEO of gambling firm Harrah's, is particularly unusual as a CEO idea practitioner, having previously been a Harvard Business School professor. CEOs usually have to get behind an idea eventually if it's going to succeed. But the original adherents and evangelists of business ideas are usually found lower in the organization. They're heads of operational business units and business functions, planners and strategists, and even individual contributors. They get things done through passion and persuasion more than power.

We'll celebrate these idea practitioners throughout this book, and more than any other subject, we are writing about them. We've interviewed more than fifty idea practitioners for this book (see appendix B for a list), and we scatter their comments throughout it. Chapter 2 is expressly about idea practitioners. We're sure that by the end of this book, you'll have read the vast majority of what has ever been said about becoming an idea practitioner and using business ideas to help organizations.

Why Now?

We believe that the subject of idea management in business is more important now than it has ever been, for at least three reasons. First, the size of the idea management problem seems to be increasing. Considerable evidence points to an onslaught of business ideas. There are more and more idea creators with an interest in propagating new business ideas: academics, consultants, journalists—even lawyers and investment bankers. And the lines between these professions become ever more blurred. The worldwide consulting industry grew at about 20 percent a year in the 1990s and early 2000s, to about $118 billion in 2002.[15] Business schools continue to grow and prosper, even in a difficult economy; in fact, student applications to leading schools are up substantially. The business advice industry is one of the fastest-growing segments of the economy (chapter 5). More people are pushing more ideas at managers than ever before. And economic uncertainty—always with us, but more so at some times than at others—makes managers even more anxious to improve their firms' performance and therefore more open to people and firms with ideas to sell. Demand creates supply, and supply creates demand.

The business press also substantially stokes the business idea marketplace. The old reliable business journals and magazines— *Harvard Business Review, Fortune, Forbes,* and *Business Week*—have been augmented by *Business 2.0, Fast Company, Forbes ASAP, CIO, CFO, Strategy and Business, Business and Strategy,* and others. Some Internet-oriented publications died in the dot-com crash and subsequent advertising drought, but there are still far too many business publications for anyone to read. Even the stable publications have increased their output of ideas. *Harvard Business Review,* for example, has doubled its frequency, from six to twelve issues per year.

In addition to more providers of ideas and more channels, it appears that the pace of ideas has accelerated since the 1980s. Quality management and TQM, for example, were pursued for well over ten years. Reengineering was popular for only about five years. Electronic commerce had only about three years in the limelight. If a practicing manager intends to capitalize on the rhetorical energy granted an idea by the press and the idea propagation industry, there is less time to do so. This all takes place at a time when the management attention to deal with new ideas is increasingly scarce—because organizations get leaner and leaner, and because the information flow within organizations is ever faster. These trends put a premium on selecting the right ideas for an organization. There is little time for addressing inappropriate ideas.

A third reason that the time is right for idea management is that innovative business ideas have become more important to companies' products and services. Manufacturing goods have become increasingly commoditized because of globalization and national overcapacity. As a result, companies in sophisticated economies seek differentiation by offering "solutions," rather than only products. The solutions are typically bundles of products, services, and ideas that together can solve business problems. A company selling customer relationship management (CRM) software, for example, might offer not only a software package, but also some services to implement the software. At the top of the market offering, the company might sell a set of ideas around improving the total customer experience. The software itself might be sourced from a low-cost producer in India, but the total package for achieving the idea might still come from Western providers. Ideas are often used to differentiate services in general, and certainly most developed economies have seen a pronounced shift to services since around the 1980s. This trend will only grow stronger in the future.

A couple of companies provide great examples of this shift to ideas within companies. Xerox remade itself as "The Document Company" when copiers and other office equipment began to become commoditized. Dan Holtshouse, one of the idea practitioners we've interviewed and worked with, helped Xerox figure out what it meant to be a document company versus a copier company and even what is meant by the concept of *document* (see sidebar). One implication of the document-company idea was that the company began to offer document processing services to corporate clients. This service is today one of Xerox's most successful businesses.

Dan Holtshouse, Idea Practitioner

Dan Holtshouse began his work career as a systems engineer, helping to develop a navigation system for the Apollo spaceflights. Since the early 1970s, however, he has helped Xerox navigate its way through changing generations of document technology. His greatest strength as an idea practitioner is in connecting business and management ideas, such as document and knowledge management, to Xerox's products and communications strategy.

Holtshouse has a master's degree in electrical engineering and an M.B.A. He has worked in several product groups within Xerox, both mainstream—copier development, graphics workstations, and printing systems—and the more "fringe" areas of start-ups. From a business ideas standpoint, his most important move was into the Corporate Communications and Strategic Development organization, a headquarters group with the mission of uncovering strategic ideas that could advance Xerox's business. It was out of this group that Xerox's long-standing label, The Document Company, was born.

This seminal idea came forth in the early 1990s, but Holtshouse considers it still relevant to Xerox and its customers: "It incorporates not only technology, but also issues of the processes and nature of work, and the nature of information and knowledge." Holtshouse was a member of a small group that put together a series of document symposia within Xerox to flesh out the concept of the document positioning. "We were successful in helping Xerox to understand what it means to focus on the document, rather than the printed page alone," he notes.

Holtshouse then evolved from focusing on documents to focusing on knowledge. He was involved in the earliest days of thinking and discussion about knowledge management. Paul Allaire, then Xerox's CEO, bought into Holtshouse's focus on knowledge and knowledge work. The CEO designated the knowledge issue as one of a few strategic issues to be emphasized in the Corporate Strategy office. To Holtshouse and Xerox, knowledge management was not just an internal concept, but rather a new market space for Xerox products and services.

Holtshouse is continuing to help Xerox adapt ideas to meet the needs of the marketplace. His current focus is on knowledge worker productivity. He is looking at how new technologies, emerging work patterns, the need for cost reduction, and advances in cognitive science and neuroscience will create the knowledge workplace of the future.

The software industry is a domain in which ideas can often differentiate products, and in some cases, a software program can serve as the mechanism of distribution for an idea. i2 Technologies, a leader in software for supply-chain management and optimization, is a prime example of this phenomenon. Sanjiv Sidhu, the CEO of i2, notes, "We believe our business is about embedding ideas in software." Sidhu cofounded the business with Ken Sharma, then a fellow engineer at Texas Instruments. The two men became devotees of the Theory of Constraints, a set of supply-chain ideas laid out by Elihu Goldratt in popular books such as *The Goal*. Sidhu and Sharma concluded that they could not visit enough companies themselves to embed the theories into businesses, but if they wrote software enabling the ideas, the ideas could be much more widely disseminated. i2 is now a billion-dollar software company, and despite Sharma's untimely death, the Theory of Constraints is becoming pervasive in companies with complex supply chains.

Like software, consulting is another industry that disseminates ideas along with its primary services. In fact, consulting is one of the industries most responsible for both creating and propagating business ideas in the marketplace. Consultants from large firms to boutiques to solo practitioners are also a frequently relied-upon source of implementation help for new business ideas. In fact, we'd argue that using a competent consulting organization is often an attractive alternative to internal implementation when management needs outstanding execution, in terms of both timing and quality. However, since we are consultants as well as researchers, we will leave it to others to perform an objective study of the role of consultants in furthering business and management ideas.

What's to Come in This Book

In this chapter, we've tried to set the tone for why business ideas and idea practitioners are important, and what high-level philosophies are critical to getting value from them. The only data we've brought to the table thus far is our historical analysis of Westinghouse and GE. Otherwise, we've presented our own observations and some quotations from knowledgeable people.

In chapters 2, 3, and 4, we'll discuss the three key components of the business idea game. Chapter 2 addresses the most important players in the idea game—the idea practitioners. These men and women make ideas a reality within companies; chapter 2 is devoted to their characteristics and perspectives. Next are the ideas themselves, the subject of chapter 3. We'll discuss how ideas can either go wrong, when they become faddish, or go right, when they become pervasive within an organization. We'll draw on this knowledge of business ideas throughout the rest of the book. Chapter 4 describes the key source of business ideas: business gurus—the people who create business ideas for a living.

Chapters 5 and 6 describe different aspects of how ideas become important and valued. Chapter 5 focuses on the interplay between markets and ideas. It describes how a practicing manager can understand the dynamics at work in idea markets and their channels of distribution. Chapter 6 discusses how to evaluate the ideas you encounter in these markets for fit with your company, using criteria such as translatability and timing. It then offers practitioners an approach to selling ideas into their own organization.

Chapters 7 and 8 present detailed case studies of how ideas work in organizations. They tell the stories of business process reengineering and knowledge management. Although we were involved in the two case studies that we describe, we did not pick them for self-aggrandizement. We picked them because they provide important examples of the different roads that business ideas can take. We'll describe what went right, what went wrong, and, most important, how these two business ideas provide lessons for getting value from those to come.

We conclude the book with chapter 9, on the role of leaders in idea-based change and a detailed interview with an outstanding idea practitioner, Steve Kerr. Described at the beginning of this chapter in his role as a leading idea practitioner at GE, Kerr is now playing the same role at Goldman Sachs. His own career and his relationship with idea-oriented leaders can be an inspiration to businesspeople considering becoming idea practitioners or idea leaders in their own organizations.

2

THE IDEA PRACTITIONERS

WHO INTRODUCES IDEAS
TO ORGANIZATIONS?

Idea practitioners are the most important players in the entire process of importing and implementing new ideas into businesses. They are the link between ideas and action. Without them, new ideas would remain on the periphery of organizations and would never get embedded into practice. Furthermore, the ideas wouldn't be nearly as useful. These managers aren't passive recipients of fully shaped ideas. The good idea practitioners all filter, add to, or subtract from the ideas they implement, "fitting" them to their organizations' specific needs. In many cases, it is from these individuals and their organizations that the gurus actually get their ideas and case examples.

We define idea practitioners as individuals who use business improvement ideas to bring about change in organizations. At some point in their careers they may have had managerial responsibility for achieving this objective. Although they may become consultants or academics sometime in their lives, they have worked for "real" companies or government agencies as well.

Even when idea practitioners are pontificating or generating new ideas themselves, it's usually on the basis of their own experience.

Let's dismiss any negative stereotypes you may hold about these individuals. They're not fad mongers, but thoughtful and reflective managers capable of distinguishing good ideas from bad. They aren't only interested in riding ideas into higher positions within their companies. Some, in fact, have felt that they could have been more successful in traditional terms had they been less passionate about ideas. These people are not head-in-the-clouds, ivory-tower intellectuals; they're pragmatic businesspeople who see the possibility of a better way. And finally, they're not starry-eyed guru groupies. Although idea practitioners are typically friendly with business gurus and occasionally bring the gurus' publications—or the gurus themselves—into their organizations, the practitioners know that it takes more than even the most charismatic and brilliant guru to make an idea a reality.

Perhaps the most noble attribute of these individuals is their lack of cynicism. It's certainly easy to be cynical about the business of business ideas. The whole thing could be dismissed as faddish, or opportunism and media hype gone mad. Cynics see consultants hungry for billable hours and academics yearning for tenure and speech deals. The managers we have studied for this book, however, see through the problems of new business ideas to their true potential. They hold out a belief that people and organizations can change. They certainly see the Dilbertian aspects of the contemporary workplace that make it worthy of lampooning, but they see beyond Dilbert to the need for, and the possibility of, real change.

Surprisingly, our study found that many of these people are repeat offenders. They became involved not only in reengineering, for example, but also in quality management, knowledge management, organizational change management, and other idea-driven initiatives. Most managers were driven not by any single idea, but by the power of new ideas in general for reshaping business and work. Having seen a lot of ideas in their time, the more seasoned practitioners have a good feeling for which ideas will benefit their own companies.

Experience in shepherding one idea to implementation can help in working with another idea. Mike Burtha, for example, an idea practitioner at Johnson & Johnson, has worked with process improvement, quality management, and knowledge management at the company. He's been able to apply lessons learned in successfully championing one idea to each succeeding one: "There are a lot of things that carried over from quality to knowledge management. Of course they're both approaches to business improvement, and I formed a lot of relationships with people and business units in quality that have been beneficial to my work with knowledge. I also learned from doing quality that it's important to customize it to the environment and culture. We tailored and customized the approach to quality, calling it the Johnson & Johnson 'Signature of Quality.' In the same way, with knowledge we thought the greater business value aspects involved sharing tacit knowledge, so we labeled the initiative 'Knowledge Networking' to emphasize the focus on people."

Who Are These People?

To our knowledge, no one has written about idea practitioners, so they are largely unknown to the world. What are their backgrounds? What positions do they hold within organizations? How does one get and hold a job as an idea practitioner? Why did these people gravitate toward the world of business ideas? In this section, we'll try to answer each of these questions, using the people we interviewed as examples.

You may have wondered what one does with a B.A. in philosophy, or a Ph.D. in European history, in the commercial environment. You become an idea practitioner! Many people we interviewed had liberal arts backgrounds. Most were quite well educated and are clearly not lacking for basic brain power. One interviewee entered Harvard at age fourteen, for example, and completed a Ph.D. program at twenty. Several other people we interviewed are currently enrolled in Ph.D. programs.

Despite their education and intelligence, these individuals entered the business world in relatively prosaic roles. Perhaps not surprisingly, many were involved with information technology in their early jobs—programming or information systems analysis. Even that area offered opportunities to innovate, as one idea practitioner noted: "I was a pretty junior programmer when I started, basically. So I wasn't even thinking in terms of innovation. But within a couple of years, I started sort of bringing new ideas into the more technical side of the job. Things like structured programming and prototyping and things like that were ideas that I was the early champion of—so you know this was a long, long time ago. But then later, as my career progressed and I got into various management jobs, it became a more expected part of my particular role, of how to be a scout and a conduit for new ideas."

Many idea practitioners started with consulting firms (as one person put it, "Consulting was a way to stay in school and not declare a major") and then moved into real companies. It's also common for them to have worked for several different organizations—like business honeybees, pollinating new ideas across industries and companies.

Mark Maletz, who alternates between consulting and idea practitioner roles within firms, followed this pattern. With a Ph.D. in artificial intelligence, Maletz worked for a Coopers & Lybrand group that developed expert systems. He then played a similar role within Xerox, which was enthusiastically pursuing expert systems for commercial application at the time. Maletz then moved to American Airlines, where he headed a group that was introducing business process reengineering into the company. After a few years there, he worked as a long-term consultant to Siemens on organizational transformation issues and then worked at McKinsey as a partner for several years. He now works as an independent consultant on organizational change topics and teaches at Babson College.

Maletz also illustrates another tendency of these individuals: to move back and forth across the idea creator/user line. Idea practitioners may work with a particular company to introduce a new idea and then later write an article or a book about it. The ideas they offer are all the stronger for their having actually applied them to real organizations. When Maletz, for example, worked in expert systems and reengineering, he was largely a modifier of existing ideas—though a creative one. In the field of organizational transformation, he's both an idea user and creator, having written a well-received article in the *Harvard Business Review*. No one who knows Maletz would ever classify him as only an applier of existing ideas. In fact, like most good idea practitioners, he synthesizes ideas from a variety of thinkers and fields, and creates his own when necessary.

Steve Denning, formerly of The World Bank, is another example of a hybrid idea creator/user. His greatest success at The World Bank was in knowledge management, where he played a key role in the transition to "The Knowledge Bank." As we discuss in chapter 8, Denning was instrumental in inserting knowledge management into the basic mission of The World Bank. After several years of wrestling with the topic and effecting change (and drawing on the ideas of others, including us), he joined the ranks of management authors and wrote *The Springboard*.[1] The book describes the power of storytelling in bringing about business change. His own stories about the role of storytelling in making knowledge a core asset of The World Bank are a powerful endorsement of the technique. We'll let him tell one of his own stories later in this chapter.

Idea practitioners also tend to be boundary spanners, working across organizations as well as within them. You're likely to see these people on the agendas at conferences, as members of communities of practice, and as sponsors of multicompany research programs. As a result, they know personally the people who create management ideas and those who modify and bring them into other organizations. This knowledge is very helpful if a key aspect of your job is to identify big thinkers and determine whose ideas other organizations find useful.

If you are a boundary spanner, however, you need to be aware of two limitations. First, you often don't get organizational permission—however informal—to be a boundary spanner until you have paid your dues as an individual contributor. One of our interviewees noted, "New people come into the company—maybe right out of business school—and they think it would be really cool to go to conferences and work with external gurus. But it doesn't work that way. You have to earn your stripes as someone who can deliver on what he promises—someone who has credibility. It is fun to work outside the organization, but you have to prove that you can credibly represent the organization and actually do something with the idea when it comes inside."

None of our successful idea practitioners were right out of school. Their decades of experience had taught them how difficult it is to bring about a new business idea. They also had the seasoning to know when an idea might work in their own organizations, and the personal networks inside their companies to know whom to enlist in their efforts.

Ideally, the idea practitioner's organization legitimizes his or her status with a title. This doesn't happen very often, but we found a great example at Intel. Gene Meieran, one of Intel's leading idea practitioners, is an Intel Fellow—the firm's highest-level technical role. Meieran, with an Sc.D. in materials science from MIT, worked at Fairchild Semiconductor with Gordon Moore, Andy Grove, and other pioneers of the industry. When he came to Intel, Meieran made important contributions in semiconductor packaging. After being named a Fellow (the second person to be so designated, after Ted Hoff, who invented the microprocessor), he was free to pursue any topic, technological or not, that he felt would help the organization. All Intel Fellows—there have been forty-nine thus far—are technical visionaries, but Meieran has also worked on managerial innovation. He and Craig Barrett, now Intel's CEO (and also a materials scientist by background) introduced a quality and reliability initiative to the manufacturing organization. Meieran has also championed the modeling of manufacturing processes, supply network modeling, remote data sensing, supplier maintenance, process control methodology, the role of the Internet in manufacturing, and knowledge management. He admits that his designation as a Fellow helps him to start brushfires around a new idea: "Whether I'm right or wrong, my stuff at a minimum will get a fair hearing. Many brushfires are significant enough to grow into real 'forest fires' of innovation."

The second caution for boundary spanners is that status for idea practitioners must be gained internally rather than externally. It's critical not to spend too much time on the lecture circuit yourself unless your internal reputation is absolutely bulletproof. We have known of several people (though they don't appear in our sample) who appeared frequently at conferences to discuss their organizations' efforts at reengineering, knowledge management, customer relationship management, and so forth. Some even wrote an article or two. But when we would visit their companies and ask about these individuals, we'd get dirty looks and muttered curses in reply. Or we'd ask, "What's going on with your knowledge superhighway project, or your customer relationship reengineering?" and we'd get blank looks. These people were good at publicizing their own work, but not particularly good at making something happen. Invariably, these same people left their companies for new jobs shortly thereafter. The imbalance between their external reputations and what they'd actually accomplished inside their organizations caught up with them.

Another common attribute of effective idea practitioners is that they are focused on something besides moving up through the organization and receiving a better title and higher income. They are truly devoted to ideas as well as their own advancement and their organization's improvement.

Not that the people we interviewed aren't successful; the list included a chief financial officer (CFO) of a global corporation and a chief operating officer of a large U.S. government agency.

By any standard, these people have done well. But they are generally not CEOs. Some have admitted that they might have been more outwardly successful had they focused on accumulating power and direct reports rather than intellectual capital. Charles "Chuck" Sieloff, a successful executive in the Information Services organization at Hewlett-Packard, was one of those people:

> At a number of points, I had career choices where the logical path might have been more responsibility but a more operational kind of job. I tended to stay away from those and to stay in jobs that gave me a little more freedom and a little more opportunity for creativity rather than managing big operational organizations. I would say there were two or three points in my career— fairly widely scattered points—where those were clear branches, and I had what some people would have considered to be a big career opportunity. But it was in a role that I didn't find very interesting, and I chose not to take those paths. I never felt handicapped by that; those were decisions that I made. One of the nice things about HP was that I always felt that those decisions were well respected and rewarded. As I made those decisions, I was given more and more discretionary time and budget to do the kind of thing that I thought made sense.

Sieloff's remarks reflect the idea practitioners' tendency to work in staff roles more than line. This is a risky place to be in contemporary business, where organizations have become "lean and mean" and where working directly with customers is the only safe place to be in a downturn. To survive in this environment, idea practitioners must constantly add value to their organizations. They must also be nimble in moving from one topic to another as management fashions come and go. Dave Barrow at BP, for example, has worked on a variety of special projects involving government relations, network computing, crisis management, capital productivity improvement, human resource processes in engineering, and knowledge management.

Finally, a word about the personalities of the idea practitioners we identified. Even though they are passionate about their ideas, they are neither zealots nor true believers. Most seem quite mild-mannered at first blush. Several said that they attribute their success in part to their reasonableness: "Cultivating a moderate image is important," one noted. "Lecturers and zealots always fail." Several also explained that they tried to ensure that the idea, and its success in the enterprise, didn't get tangled up in their own personalities. Hubert Saint-Onge, the executive at Canadian insurer Clarica whom we profile at the end of this chapter, argues that idea practitioners should "allow organizations to reach their own conclusions, and become invisible" to the process as individuals. Chris Hoenig, who advocated for business ideas at the U.S. General Accounting Office and then headed a small software firm, believes that there is a "critical mass of capabilities" for an "ideas person." His view is that such an individual should be serious, credible, earnest, and passionate. He or she should also exhibit a "sense of discipleship" and have a strong sense of direction for his or her own career and for what will make the organization successful.

What Do These People Do with Ideas?

Of course, every idea practitioner is different, as are their organizations and the ideas they propound. But we found a surprising degree of commonality in how these individuals go about their idea-based leadership. The rough process that they follow is described in the following sections and in greater detail in later chapters. It is depicted serially, although a given idea may skip or repeat a step here and there, or follow a different order.

Scan for and Identify the Idea

The first step for these idea practitioners is to identify an idea worth pursuing. As we've discussed, these ideas don't come prepackaged; almost all our idea practitioners filter and synthesize from multiple ideas and modify them for their organization's need. Several managers reported that they feel the need for an interdisciplinary approach to business thought leadership.

One bit of evidence for an interdisciplinary approach to new ideas is that idea practitioners consulted multiple external sources and worked with multiple external thought leaders. They read many business magazines, including *Harvard Business Review, Sloan Management Review, Fortune, Fast Company,* and others. One long-term idea practitioner, Lawrence Baxter at Wachovia Corporation, believes that a manager should look even beyond the business literature, which is very limited. One time when we interviewed him, for example, he was reading a book on super string theory in physics.

Carol Bekar, who helped introduce new information and knowledge management ideas to Bristol-Myers Squibb, argues that if people are going to read business books, they should consult relatively timeless ones, not books that become rapidly dated. She cites works by Peter Drucker as examples. She also believes it's important to consult sources from outside your own country. She personally reads *The Economist* for a non-U.S. point of view. Reuben Slone, a Whirlpool executive currently in charge of logistics and supply chain management, believes that printed sources—particularly the *Harvard Business Review*—are a good place to start, but that further research on the Internet is important for determining whether an idea is suitable for adoption.

Because academic and other external relationships are important sources of ideas for idea practitioners, these businesspeople are the most likely participants in management conferences, workshops, and multiclient research programs. Idea practitioners are also the mainstays of industry-sponsored research programs at business schools. At times they even have university affiliations.

Gene Meieran at Intel, for example, has extensive university affiliations. As the company's senior sponsor for its relationships with MIT, he works with both the business and engineering schools there. Special programs such as the Media Lab and the joint business and engineering program Leaders for Manufacturing are other MIT-affiliated projects under Meieran's sponsorship. At one point, he served as director of research for the program and had a faculty designation. Meieran also sits on the board of advisors for the Materials Engineering Department at Purdue University and the dean's board of advisors at the University of New Mexico. The University of California at Berkeley, Stanford University, and the University of Michigan are other stomping grounds (idea-gathering spots) for Meieran. He (and Intel) also get many good ideas from the company's sponsorship of the Intel International Science and Engineering Fairs (Intel ISEF), in which high school students compete for scholarships.

In some cases, individuals may arrive at a company with a particular idea in mind. They may even have been recruited for that reason. Reuben Slone of Whirlpool came to the auto parts manufacturer Federal-Mogul after stints as a consultant with Ernst & Young and EDS. His role at Federal-Mogul was to lead reengineering and other approaches to process change. An early adopter of these approaches as a consultant, he was brought in to lead the initiatives because of his expertise. Since then, however, Reuben has evolved his role, taking responsibility for e-business and then logistics at Whirlpool after leaving Federal-Mogul.

In other cases, individuals are not trying to push a particular idea. Several of the managers we interviewed testified to the benefits of knowing the organization well before attempting to fit an idea to it. Some of the relevant dimensions include the company's age and whether the company is low-tech or high, mature or young, competitive or not competitive. Giora Hadar, who has been involved in several new change programs at the U.S. Federal Aviation Administration (FAA), notes that the cultural prongs of the FAA are "safety and system efficiency." It's a conservative organization, and ignoring these dimensions when introducing a new program is a recipe for failure.

Several of the managers we interviewed described a process in which they try to anticipate new approaches to business before they are fully developed. Debbie Smith, who leads a thought leadership group at State Street Bank and Trust Co., describes the process in brief: "It's trying to be on point or anticipatory of

trends and issues—market trends and market issues, business issues—from a strategic perspective and then conveying that information back to our people internally or being engaged in dialogue with our clients through forums or what have you."

Indeed, several of our interviewees noted that there was a
strong sense of "alreadyness" in their reaction to ideas others
might perceive as new. Carol Bekar commented that when people began to write about knowledge management in the mid-
1990s, it was consistent with both her own beliefs and initiatives
she already had under way within the research community at
Bristol-Myers Squibb. And when articles and books on the management of attention began to emerge in 2001, Chuck Sieloff at
HP wasn't surprised. He'd been thinking about the issue for several years, had begun initiatives at HP to address the issue, and
had even written an article on the topic.

What do these idea practitioners do when articles or books
come out on topics they've already been thinking about? Not surprisingly, they use the materials and their authors to their own
advantage and that of their organizations. They'll circulate the article internally or bring in the author to speak. We found little
pride of ownership among these managers. Since their goal is to
get something done with an idea, they'll typically embrace any
external resource that can help to bring credibility or best practice. We will have more to say on the topic of external credibility
in chapter 5, and more on the issues of filtering and fitting ideas
to the organization in chapter 6.

Package the Idea

Later in the book, we will talk about the language used in
describing new ideas. Language is one aspect of how businesspeople package an idea to make it appealing and more likely to succeed. Joe McCrea, the U.K. government's director of "Knowledge-
Enhanced Government," and a long-term researcher and adviser
to cabinet members in the Labour government, has given considerable thought to how to package an idea—and how to remember

its essence. The following four points came from his response to our questions:

- First and most important, keep your eyes on the prize. Have a clear idea in your own head about the ultimate possibility for your idea if everything went perfectly. And then work back with the hundreds of steps that you will need to take to attain perfection. As long as you're continuing to take those steps, however distant the ultimate prize is, you're progressing on your way.

- Keep the description of your idea very, very simple. Dressing it up in lots of fancy words and jargon might impress the ranks of the initiated, but it won't attract, motivate, or inspire Joe Bloggs. Also, don't forget that many people may wish to oppose you and will totally underestimate anything that isn't dressed up in fancy language and jargon. So, the more radical the idea, the more matter-of-factly you should describe it.

- Don't spell out the full ultimate significance of your idea unless and until you absolutely have to. Grand designs set out at the outset of your idea might be a great boost to your own ego, but they also tend to attract the fainthearted and potential enemies before your idea is mature enough to fend for itself. A truly radical idea is like a small child. It needs to be protected and nurtured in the beginning.

- If you can, break down your big idea into lots of little ideas, and set them running in the organization. This is what a friend of mine called "Trojan mice." They will naturally coalesce over time without your overt intervention.

Of course, it's possible to oversimplify (or overshrink) an idea. Hubert Saint-Onge, a senior manager and idea practitioner at Clarica until 2002, summarizes the risk this way: "I don't do T-shirts." Reducing complicated ideas to short slogans may work in some organizations, but it's more likely to create misunderstandings and false expectations.

Several idea practitioners also warned specifically against packaging new ideas in terms of the technologies used to implement them. "Have a social focus, not a technology one." "Never advocate a technology—advocate process, people, and content." "Technology is always linked to overselling. It should be positioned as an enabler." It's interesting that although many managers had technological credentials, they chose to de-emphasize them.

Advocate the Idea

No business idea takes root within an organization purely on its own merits. Instead it has to be sold—to senior executives, to the rank and file, to middle managers. Our idea practitioners spend a great deal of time and effort on the advocacy of the idea—on packaging it up and selling it around their organizations.

The simplest, most straightforward aspect of advocacy is to seek senior executive support. The CEO is, of course, the most desirable sponsor. According to one idea practitioner, "ideas that get CEO support get implemented. Those that don't, don't." But in our own experience, it's not always that simple. We can recall ideas whose names had never crossed the CEO's lips (knowledge management at Hewlett-Packard, for example), but were still successful, at least up to a point. On the other hand, some ideas enjoyed CEO support, but eventually died anyway. At Xerox, for example, the idea of reengineering died because of a particularly entrenched middle management bureaucracy and a CEO (that is, the president of the largest business unit) who left the organization and was succeeded by a nonbeliever. Eventually, however, any new business idea will need CEO-level support if it's going to have a big impact on the organization.

One of the critical success factors in advocacy is to link the idea to something the organization already cares about and can easily understand. For example, Antonella Padova, who led knowledge management efforts at Whirlpool, knew that the senior management of the company—particularly the CEO—passionately believed that innovation was going to be a key factor in Whirlpool's future success. The firm could no longer make commodity home appliances; it had to be innovative in its products and services. When Padova was advocating for knowledge management, she realized that the way to get buy-in for the topic was to tie it to innovation. There is a natural linkage between the issues anyway, and Padova certainly believed that a strong knowledge orientation would be conducive to innovation. But to be successful, you have to be flexible and ride a train that's already leaving the station.

Idea practitioners have to use all the tools at their disposal. If they can enlist others on the outside or the inside and build coalitions to advance their ideas, they should do so. This is particularly important when the idea practitioner is trying to influence several higher levels in the organizational hierarchy. Josh Plaskoff, knowledge management consultant at Eli Lilly and Company, describes how he used help from an outside executive to persuade internal executives about the virtues of knowledge management:

> *I knew the president of a big corporate university who was interested in the knowledge management work that I was doing. . . . I called him and said, "I need your help. I'm flying some executives up on a benchmarking trip to talk to you about training and development. What I want you to do is get them interested in knowledge management." He agreed. We then discussed what he could say to generate more interest in knowledge management. So our executives flew there assuming that all they were going to hear about was training and development. Instead they heard that training was not the only solution; the corporate university had made a significant investment in knowledge management. The university president and his staff not only described their knowledge management activities, but also encouraged our executives to look at some of the knowledge management work,*

which the university president had taken an interest in, that was beginning to surface at our company. They came back from the trip really high on knowledge management. I could not have gotten them to this level of excitement alone.

At times our managers have enlisted consultants to help sell their messages. Outsiders have credibility that insiders sometimes don't. Some use consultants to bring in ideas, but more frequently they referred to consultants as a means of emphasizing ideas they already had. One manager described consultants as being almost like ventriloquists. He would give them the words, and the consultant would pass them around the organization. Consultants can also help by being a private sounding board for the formulation of the idea, and by gathering materials and evidence in support of it. As consultants ourselves, we'd suggest using these resources not just as a mouthpiece, but as a partner in shaping the idea and evangelizing for it.

Make It Happen

The business of implementation is less about ideas than about managing people, budgets, projects, and processes. One company for which the topic of "making it happen" comes up frequently is General Electric. Perhaps that's why the company has been so successful at idea-based change. As mentioned in chapter 1, the company has a well-defined system (in GE terminology, its Operating System) of management meetings, planning sessions, and reviews to ensure that ideas get put into practice all around the company. For one of the company's more recent idea-driven initiatives—the idea of e-business, or digitization—several steps helped drive implementation:

- Jack Welch's announcement that each business had to explain how it would become the e-business leader in its industry at a forthcoming strategy review.

- Speeches from external e-business leaders (including Joe Liemandt of Trilogy, Scott McNealy of Sun Microsystems, and Lou Gerstner of IBM) at meetings of GE executives.

- The requirement to identify an e-business leader in each business unit by a staffing review meeting, supported by a "Destroy Your Business.com" task force to identify key e-business threats.

- Support from GE's chief information officer (CIO), Gary Reiner, who also headed the twenty-person Corporate Initiatives Group.

- A mentoring program in which each of GE's top five hundred executives were to identify an Internet mentor, preferably under thirty years old.

- Frequent visits from Welch, in which he asked local leaders whether they were up to speed on e-business.[2]

Given all these implementation mechanisms, how could GE not succeed with e-business ideas?

Outside GE, our idea practitioners offered several pieces of advice from which aspiring idea practitioners could benefit:

- Ideas need to show a quick payoff, so keep track of financial costs and benefits.

- A fast win may actually be a loss; major change involves working on foundations, which takes time.

- Every idea needs an implementation plan if it's going to go anywhere.

- Tie the execution of the idea into performance appraisals and promotions.

- Experiment, then scale up.

- Unqualified successes are those in which the new ideas are useful to individual workers' jobs (so the fit has to be perfect, or the idea or the job must be redesigned).

- At some point, you have to know when to get out of the way and let others execute.

A key implementation issue is whether and when to create a specialized function to promote and manage the idea. Some ideas in the late twentieth century and early twenty-first have led to well-established functions. Many firms, for example, had functions oriented to the management of quality; fewer for reengineering. The number of organizations with knowledge management functions and so-called chief knowledge officers may still be on the rise. What kinds of ideas require a dedicated organization, and where within the company should it reside?

We have no generic answer to the question, but only some rules of thumb. A dedicated organization is often useful at early stages of implementation. Before an idea becomes well understood across the organization, it will benefit from a collection of experts and facilitators. Another perspective is that where a business idea starts out is less important than where it ends up in the long run. It makes sense that the quality-management idea started in the manufacturing organization, for example, but there might be a problem if it remained there over time. A lack of movement of the quality-management idea would indicate that other parts of the organization didn't seize upon quality as something important for them too. Similarly, knowledge management may have arisen naturally within the information technology department, but this new idea should not stay there forever. Perhaps the best situation is when a new idea originates within a specific related functional area, then moves as a corporate function reporting to a general manager, then becomes eliminated or highly diminished as the idea becomes embedded within the entire business. In many firms, quality is now part of everyone's job, not just the province of a particular function or department.

Firms that don't wish to create a permanent function or group to implement an idea may choose to outsource it. The concept of "business process outsourcing" suggests that virtually any organizational capability can be offered by an external provider for however long it is needed.

Take the Idea Outside

In the best of all possible worlds of business ideas, new approaches would first be implemented internally and then taken externally as a product or service. Six Sigma quality tools, for example, could be embedded not just into internal processes, but into services for customers (as is the case in General Electric's Services Network). A professional services firm could sell knowledge management directly to its clients, rather than only selling hours (as did Ernst & Young with its "Ernie" online knowledge offering).

The external transfer of ideas doesn't just happen automatically. Someone has to consciously look for opportunities to take ideas outside. At State Street Bank and Trust Co., for example, Debbie Smith was asked to lead a group that takes new financial and business improvement ideas directly to customers: "I was asked to take a different position and not do sales so much as look at thought leadership, more strategic marketing. But again, [I was supposed to consider it] as it related to our clients—as a way to further integrate ourselves or further tighten our relationship with our clients. The goal is to really be top of mind, or understand top-of-mind issues for clients that we could address internally, as well as translate into relevant practices or products or services that we could provide. In doing that, I essentially tried to create a platform that was communicating trends and ideas and so forth through a variety of vehicles."

Perhaps the best example of taking a business improvement idea into the marketplace is at The World Bank. Knowledge management began as an internal business improvement approach and became the core of the organization's mission. How did this transformation take place? Steve Denning kindled the idea of knowledge management at The World Bank and stayed with it through the external transformation:

I started telling narratives about knowledge in the course of being considered for the job of chief information officer in The World Bank. It started to reverberate with some of the vice presidents. They started saying, "Look, this is exciting, we've got to do it," and there was excitement at the working level. Then the management got worried that here's this guy who's starting to get all our motion behind this idea. So then they announced that there wasn't going to be a chief information officer; the whole selection process was closed down. I was told to go back to my office and stop causing trouble. But then some of the vice presidents who had been behind it said, "This is crazy. This is the most important idea around; we've got to keep going." And so they invited me to show how we would implement this idea in all the vice presidencies.

That went on for a couple of months, and the thing was gathering momentum and they were ready to put money behind it. But in July of 1996, management got frightened again, so they told the vice presidents to stop it: "Forget it, it's not going to happen, it's irrelevant." So I went away again.

Then in September 1996, I was still conniving with the vice presidents, and it was obvious, we [had] to do this, [it was] the future! We were talking about ideas such as, "Suppose we could get Wolfensohn [James Wolfensohn, president of The World Bank] to announce this at the annual meeting?" I was actually sitting in the office with one of these vice presidents on a Wednesday afternoon. We finally decided, "Well, it's too complicated, and the annual meeting's only two weeks away. We've got all these centurion guards surrounding the president. If we try it and run we might make it through, but there would be horrible punishment. So why don't we just wait until after the annual meeting? And when things are calm and when nobody's noticing, we'll try to make a run."

We always thought that if we could get ten minutes in front of the president, that would be it, he would buy it, and we'd be off. But getting the ten minutes was the problem. So we're sitting in the vice president's office, and the phone rings. It turns out [to be] Wolfensohn. He's in a traffic jam in New York, and he's on his cell phone. He's reading the annual meeting speech, and he tells the vice president, "Well, this is crap—surely there's one good idea in the whole organization," and the vice president [says], "Well, as a matter of fact there is."

In ten minutes, he gives him the whole idea, and Wolfensohn says, "That's great, I'll get back to you." He goes into the meeting, he tries it out, and they say it's a fabulous idea. He comes in the next day, and the vice president and I are asked to draft his speech, so we spend the night drafting it. The next day, he's giving the speech to the board of directors, saying that this the new strategy in The World Bank. The week after that, he's announcing at the annual meeting, in front of 170 finance ministers and their entourages that this is the strategy: We're going to become "The Knowledge Bank"; we're going to share our knowledge with the world.

When the centurion guards heard all this, they were horrified. This was the worst-case scenario. I mean, one of them had even told me that I was never to talk to Wolfensohn, because he would probably buy it. So now we talked to him; now he's bought it.

This was when the fighting got really rough, when they started to use real bullets instead of rubber bullets, because now [there was] a real question that the thing might actually happen. Nevertheless, they thought that it would blow away, so I was sort of given a temporary appointment for one year or two. I was supposed to muddle along, keep Wolfensohn happy, and pretend that something was happening. [They hoped that] then he'd forget about it, and then the organization could move on. But it didn't.[3]

Denning's story suggests that persistence, political savvy, and access to senior executives play an important role in getting ideas from the inside of the organization to the outside. It's natural that the stakes for business ideas that become embedded into products, services, and missions of organizations would be substantially higher than those employed internally. Denning speaks amusingly of the "centurion guards" at The World Bank, but no large organization is without them—senior managers who are happy with the status quo and who don't want new ideas that would threaten it coming in from left field. For anyone to assume that putting new business ideas in place isn't difficult and politically charged is naïve at best. A professor friend of ours once aptly described the issue when told by a young M.B.A. that his career ambition was to be a "reengineer." The professor replied, "That's like a career as a second lieutenant in a field artillery unit."[4] In other words, it's likely to be a short career.

Profiles of Three Idea Practitioners

For the final section of this chapter, we'll profile three idea practitioners we consider particularly noteworthy for one reason or another. Their capabilities have translated into tremendous success and positions of great responsibility, yet they maintain a focus on ideas. We present them as role models for anyone who wants to lead with ideas.

Blythe McGarvie

The stereotype of the CFO is a hard-nosed, green-eye-shaded penny-pincher who can only evaluate new business ideas in terms of their internal rate of return. But Blythe McGarvie, the CFO at Société BIC (the well-known maker of pens, razors, etc.) is not your typical CFO. We first met her at a conference on new business ideas, sponsored by Harvard Business School Press. At this meeting, where CFOs were hardly common, McGarvie explained her drive: "Business is about the intellectual challenge.

That's what I thrive on and what I look for in the people I hire." Her search for intellectual stimulation and a broad perspective has also led her to join three companies' boards of directors, including Accenture's.

McGarvie may have a somewhat typical educational background for a CFO, having majored in economics as an undergraduate and having received an M.B.A. from the Kellogg School at Northwestern University. Her path diverged from that of most other future CFOs at Kellogg, however, when she focused her studies on both accounting and marketing. Although McGarvie did become a CPA and worked for a global accounting firm for a few years, she says, "I'm not a typical accountant." She demonstrated this with her next job, becoming a brand manager at Kraft Foods. That boundary-spanning background is typical of many idea practitioners, as is her family's academic focus: McGarvie is married to a professor and is the daughter of a professor and a teacher. The mixture of marketing and finance served her well when she became CFO of Hannaford Brothers, a progressive, Maine-based grocery retailer. She then moved to BIC when Hannaford was acquired by another firm.

McGarvie sees herself as playing two roles relative to ideas within BIC. One is to bring in new ideas, both financial and otherwise. She reads widely, attends conferences, and serves on outside boards in order to scan for new ideas and identify which ones might make sense at BIC. In her short time there since 1999, she's already imported some new approaches to taxation, transfer pricing, and reporting to the company. McGarvie also sees herself as helping to shape a new culture at BIC, which is a relative novelty for a French firm. "I'm trying to bring a discipline of closure," she notes. "What's the next step? There's a strong oral culture in French business that may not ever get to what needs to be done to make something happen."

Her other role is to influence the way ideas get circulated around the organization. "I'm trying to break the conspiracy of silence that's often found in hierarchical French firms. For example, we organized an annual CFO and Technology Conference, with eighty people attending from around the world. I insisted that each person attending come up with an idea to improve our business. Nobody had ever asked them before! But I walk away with several really good ideas every time we have the conference." She also tries not to throw cold water on other people's ideas, even when she considers the ideas not very good. "I don't want to be the hard-nosed evaluator. I do apply objective criteria in evaluating ideas—it's part of my identity as a finance person—but I try to put a little candy around my opinions so that people will still volunteer ideas."

McGarvie sees the filtering out of inappropriate ideas for her organization as an important role of the idea practitioner: "If the idea isn't right for the culture or the pacing of the organization, it won't fly." One idea that she believes probably isn't right for BIC now, for example, is EVA, or economic value added. "It's not a bad set of ideas—in fact, they're great for the right organization. But it's not a good fit to the pace of our organization and French financial reporting structures."

In a traditional French firm, an American female CFO new to the company might have a difficult time getting the credibility she would need to bring about change. But McGarvie has the strong support of CEO Bruno Bich, who brought her into the job and wants change in the organization. "Bruno's support helps a lot—he's the ultimate insider, and his name is on the company." She also brought in an entirely new team for the finance function, which lets her concentrate on bringing about the kinds of changes BIC needs.

McGarvie would seem to be a prime candidate for headhunters seeking a CEO. But like many idea practitioners, she says that more power is not her goal: "Becoming a CFO was my dream, and I attained that at age thirty-nine. My next goal is to share my ideas, mentor young people, maybe even write a column or book." It's a logical objective for many idea practitioners.

Dave Clarke

We first met Dave Clarke when he was effectively the CIO of W. L. Gore and Associates, a $1 billion-plus company that makes GORE-TEX, Glide dental floss, neurosurgery suture sealant, and lots of other products from the chemical molecule polytetrafluoroethylene. We say "effectively" because Gore has no official titles; it's the best example we've seen of a fluid, self-organizing company in the flesh. Gore thrives on ideas, and self-organization is only one of them. Clarke himself might have been referred to as the "chief idea officer" while he worked there, having introduced such notions as knowledge management, enterprise systems, systems engineering, and even a formal information technology (IT) function to Gore. He also actively advocated and discussed ideas outside the IT function, including several related to product development, R&D, and global management. In an attempt to improve communications, he once banned PowerPoint presentations among his team members.

Clarke says that Gore was a great training ground for anyone in the business of introducing new ideas: "Gore had a weird dichotomy in terms of people's freedom [to do] or not to do things. You could certainly get ideas to catch fire quickly if you could really convince people that it was a great idea. It was also almost impossible to move someone who was entrenched in the opposite direction, because there was no organizational pressure for them to move. What I found there—and I think it works well elsewhere too—is that you try to sell at all levels. You have to get senior leadership buy-in, and you also have to get grassroots buy-in."

But as a highly decentralized firm, Gore had a limited tolerance for ideas that crossed the company. Clarke decided to accept a job at the other extreme of size and decentralization, becoming director of IT operations and infrastructure at General Motors North America. In that job, he managed more than $1 billion of IT infrastructure and helped transform GM from a lumbering giant to the increasingly successful firm it is today. He was able to implement some new ideas at GM, including an innovation in IT project reporting that was described as a case study in a prominent technology publication.[5] He also introduced the use of cultural anthropology to understand the take-up of new technology. This project taught him the importance of using the right metaphor when introducing a new technology or idea:

> *What I found was that we were introducing the technology in the wrong way. Sometimes it was simply things like needing more training. More often than not, though, it was this kind of reaction from a potential user of technology: "Look, you gave us a new system to use, and it doesn't make any sense. We just flat out don't like the system and it doesn't work for us." We failed to understand the user's context and background, so [the user] had no frame of reference for the new idea or system.*
>
> *Designing the system with a familiar metaphor eased the technology introduction. So I think the choice of metaphor for introducing a new idea and the kinds of cultural artifacts that you wrap around it have a lot to do with whether it's successful or not.*

Of course, GM isn't known for its receptivity to new ideas from middle managers. Clarke eventually tired of Detroit and wanted the chance to apply his ideas in a new setting with an opportunity to contribute more to society. With the intellectual restlessness typical of our idea practitioners, Clarke has now taken a similar IT job at the American Red Cross. We hope that the organization knows that it's not just getting an IT infrastructure executive.

Hubert Saint-Onge

Hubert Saint-Onge has made an organization and a career out of new business ideas. He's managed to knit such managerial innovations as customer relationship management, brand management, organizational learning, e-learning, and knowledge management into an entire corporate department that he calls Strategic Capabilities. This all took place at the Canadian insurance firm Clarica (formerly Mutual Life of Canada), a 150-year-old company acquired by Sun Life in 2002.

Saint-Onge had previously led a leadership center for Canadian Imperial Bank of Commerce (CIBC), hosting 6,500 managers a year at a residential center. Like Jack Welch at GE's Crotonville educational center, Saint-Onge was attempting to use the CIBC center as a catalyst for broad change in the bank. Then he got a call from Clarica, which was initially seeking a new head of the human resources department. He parlayed that opening into a series of discussions with Clarica CEO Bob Astley. The result was Saint-Onge's much broader role as senior vice president of strategic capabilities. The job—an idea practitioner's dream and one of the top six executive roles at the firm—includes the following functions:

- customer strategies and branding at the corporate level

- strategic planning

- building organizational capabilities, including culture, leadership, and business processes

- people management, including knowledge and learning

Much of Saint-Onge's focus while at Clarica was on issues around knowledge and learning. He became one of the creators of the knowledge management movement, speaking on and shaping the topic at conferences and informal gatherings of the early knowledge management gurus. He helped push the idea toward the more tacit and community-oriented conceptions of knowledge management. Within Clarica, he led a variety of knowledge and learning initiatives that were key to the company's success. Applying knowledge management ideas to managing a large acquisition by Clarica, for example, led to the very rapid integration of the new business into the existing one. Saint-Onge also put in place a high degree of online learning materials used widely by Clarica employees.

To his other areas of responsibility, Saint-Onge also brought transformational changes. In the area of people management, he encouraged continuous learning for all employees, while moving to self-service in people management transactions. He made similar shifts in customer relationships, establishing a center for customer knowledge while shifting the focus to self-service for customer transactions. Saint-Onge was also heavily involved in the shift to the new name and brand Clarica—and the change from a mutual to a stock company—all of which has a much more exciting set of connotations than "Mutual Life of Canada."

Saint-Onge brought substantial change to Clarica, but he was always concerned that the changes were broadly owned within the organization. He came to this approach through experience: "One of the problems that I had with my prior job was that a lot of my work was much too idiosyncratic. A lot was too focused on me as a person; my profile was much too high. When I left there, the whole place in fact collapsed over a period of eighteen months. This is not what you want to do! You can't go into something with the level of commitment that I bring to this work and feel that the moment you leave, everything collapses behind you. I had been extremely mindful in this job of building it in such a way that it's more of a web. A web of ideas, collectively owned."

The transformation at Clarica was successful, raising its market capitalization from $2.4 billion to $6.7 billion. The company then attracted the attention of larger suitors, and it was acquired by Sun Life Financial Services in 2001. After five years of relentlessly pushing new ideas to implementation, in 2002 Saint-Onge took a new post as CEO of Konverge and Know, a firm that focuses on issues of knowledge and building strategic capabilities.

3

IDEAS AT WORK

IT'S THE CONTENT THAT COUNTS

IDEA PRACTITIONERS are obviously important to successful idea-based change, but they cannot be successful without another key resource—the ideas themselves. In this chapter, we'll talk about the attributes of new business and management ideas, and the importance of developing a perspective on them. Along the way, we'll describe our own perspective—the key principles for managing "new" business ideas—one of which is that the ideas aren't really new!

As we described in chapter 1, new business and management ideas offer the significant potential of improved business performance. If you manage people in a certain way, or think of your business in this new dimension, or plan or execute differently, or (you fill in the blank), then your business results will improve and you'll be happier and more fulfilled. Sometimes the improved performance is explicit, sometimes more implicit. Sometimes the focus is more individual, and with other ideas, it's more organizational.

ime, there are probably dozens of ideas floating
...nough the early twenty-first century seems remark-
..y short on them). Since the business idea industry started
around the beginning of the twentieth century, there have been
hundreds if not thousands of ideas put in circulation. Just to give
you a flavor, we've listed as many as we could think of—or find in
other lists—in appendix A. Of course, it's impossible to arrive at a
definitive list; one observer might combine total quality management and Six Sigma, whereas another might list them separately.

Three Classic Themes

Almost all the ideas share one or more of three business objectives: improved efficiency, greater effectiveness, and innovation in products or processes. These objectives might be described
in commonsense terms as doing things right, doing the right
thing, and doing something new. During difficult economic periods, organizations often seek ideas on how to cut costs or perform
operations more efficiently. In better times, companies are attracted to ideas that help them do their work more effectively.
Even more expansive business thinkers seek ways to identify innovative new products, services, and business opportunities.

Of course, many ideas help a company achieve multiple objectives. Knowledge management, for example, can aid organizations in becoming both more effective and more innovative.
Some of the most popular management notions can hit on all
three objectives. One reason that electronic commerce struck a
responsive chord in the late 1990s is that it seemed to enable all
three objectives. Companies could execute customer and supplier
transactions much more efficiently through the Internet than
through other channels. Certain business processes, such as marketing, could be performed more effectively with the customer
information available through the Internet. And of course, many
service and business innovations emerged through e-commerce.

FIGURE 3 - 1

Business Ideas by the Classic Three Objectives

Efficiency	Activity-based costing, activity value analysis, benchmarking, centralization, cost-benefit analysis, downsizing, EVA, economies of scale, enterprise systems, experience curves
Effectiveness	Artificial intelligence, attention management, balanced scorecard, brand management, business modeling, change management, core competence, core capabilities, corporate culture, customer relationship management, decentralization, decision trees
Innovation	Adaptive enterprises, brainstorming, chaos/complexity, concurrent engineering, creative destruction, diversification, double-loop learning, empowerment, entrepreneurship

Efficiency, effectiveness, and innovation aren't the only possible objectives—some leadership and organizational objectives are more psychological in nature, for example—but these three underlie a great many of the business-oriented goals of most management notions. In figure 3-1, we list several ideas from appendix A and classify them by the objectives they typically serve.

The Life Cycles of Ideas

Another attribute that all business ideas have in common is a life cycle, both outside and inside the organizations in which they are adopted. The biggest ideas burst on the business scene like bright comets, gathering more and more attention from the press and businesspeople. But no idea can have such intense visibility permanently; hot ideas soon cool and fade from the scene. They disappear not only from the magazines and conference agendas, but also from the internal agendas of managers within companies. Some ideas, like e-commerce, even seem to go through a period of overly negative hype after so much positive attention.

Other ideas have different trajectories. They may not get as much press attention in the first place, but may stay around longer within organizations. The topic of strategic planning doesn'tengender as much excitement today as it did in the 1980s, but according to a Bain & Company survey, it's one of the most perennially popular approaches to business improvement.[1] In the information systems world, for example, big enterprise packages like SAP, Oracle, and PeopleSoft haven't gotten nearly as much public visibility as the Internet, but they're enormously successful within large organizations, and the budgets spent on them surpass e-commerce spending within many companies.[2]

The Internal Idea Cycle

It's important to point out that the life cycle of an idea within a company is quite distinct from that in the press and the public. Many firms certainly adopt ideas as they are moving upward on the external visibility path, but they don't have to. For example, GE adopted Six Sigma quality management at an out-of-phase time relative to the external market, and prospered greatly with it. Confident organizations should adopt ideas not necessarily when other people are touting them, but when they are truly needed. We'll discuss the internal life cycle first and then move on to the external life cycle.

What does long-term success for a business idea look like within organizations? Starting at the end of the process, success looks like pervasiveness. The idea is so pervasive within the organization that it appears to be invisible. Everyone practices it without thinking about it. There are no conferences on it, no highly visible gurus, no consulting projects, perhaps not a department devoted to the idea. Conferences, gurus, and so forth, abounded during previous phases of the idea's life cycle, but now it's baked into everything that goes on.

What's an example of this level of success? We'd argue that quality and total quality management are pervasive in many companies. Even by the late 1980s, 100 percent of large U.S. companies had some quality programs in place.[3] At many of these com-

FIGURE 3-2

The P Cycle of a Successful Business Idea

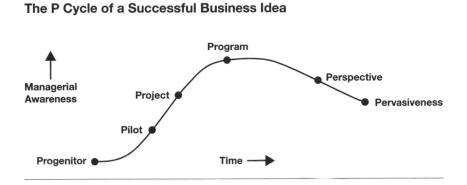

panies, quality became simply a part of "how we do business." Explicit quality programs and quality departments began to disappear as everyone adopted the ideas. A Wall Street analyst once told researchers that in the industries he covers, when he hears executives touting quality programs, he downgrades their stocks. His view is that the programs should be sufficiently pervasive that no one feels the need to talk about them.

What are the prior steps in the march of a business idea toward pervasiveness? We've identified several typical steps in figure 3-2. We call this model the P cycle, because all the steps start with that letter.

All ideas have *progenitors*. These are both the people who bring the idea into the organization and the ideas that preceded a specific idea and supplied its various components and perspectives. When the individuals are ready to articulate and advocate for a particular idea, it has reached the progenitor stage.

The first application of the idea within an organization is typically a *pilot,* usually a modest or small-scale implementation to prove that the idea can work within the organization. The intent is to learn some of the idiosyncrasies of the idea and its fit to the organization as the idea is put to work. At this point, the idea may have little budget, management support, or visibility within the organization.

A *project* is when the idea "comes out of the closet." Funding, labor, attention, and other resources begin to flow toward the idea. When an idea reaches the project stage, senior managers would know about the idea, and it begins to appear in the internal communications of the organization.

When a project is successful, it may migrate into a *program,* or a series of projects all based on the same idea. A program would generally involve many parts of the organization at once and would go on for several years. It is at the program stage that the idea has its maximum visibility and awareness levels throughout the organization. It may be discussed in external communications, such as the annual report or analyst briefings.

When programs are successful and continue over a long period, they penetrate the mind of the organization and become a *perspective.* At this point, the ideas begin to be part of everyday work life for a substantial number of individuals. People are still conscious of the idea when they practice it.

As we've discussed, *pervasiveness* is the ideal end state for a business improvement notion. It's a perspective that has gone universal and unconscious. Awareness levels are not zero, but they are well down from the project and program levels. But awareness is no longer necessary when an idea affects everyone's behavior.

The External Idea Cycle

As we've noted, the P cycle, which represents success from an individual organization's point of view, is fundamentally distinct from the external popularity cycle of an idea. External popularity includes awareness of the idea in the media, academe, and industry.

Barbara Ettorre, senior editor at the publication *Management Review,* has delineated five stages in the external life cycle of an idea. Figure 3-3 shows each stage of the external life cycle as compared with the distinct curve of the P cycle. In stage 1, the discovery stage, the idea is just beginning to enter popular awareness. Very early articles, perhaps one by a guru in *Sloan Management*

FIGURE 3 - 3

External Life Cycle of an Idea, Compared to the P Cycle

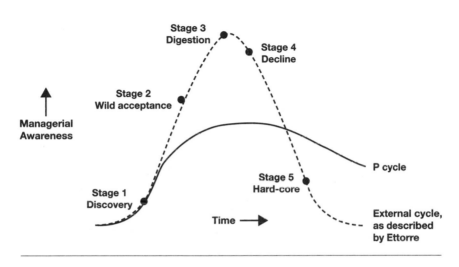

Review or a mention in the *Wall Street Journal,* appear. During stage 2 the idea becomes increasingly popular, sometimes gaining wild acceptance. During stage 3 the idea receives critical and managerial scrutiny. In stage 4, which initiates decline, the number of users begins to drop off. Only staunch, or hard-core, supporters remain loyal to the idea through stage 5.[4] For example, the discovery stage of management by objectives (MBO) was 1954 to 1964, the wild-acceptance stage was 1964 to 1981, the digestion stage 1981 to 1992, the decline stage 1992 to 1996, and the hardcore stage continues into the early twenty-first century.[5]

For any given management idea, the level of external awareness may be greater or lesser than that within a company (figure 3-3). The external life cycle for a business idea may be shorter or longer than its internal life cycle. The point is that both types of cycles exist, and an astute idea practitioner should be aware of both the internal and external positioning of an idea at a given time.

The cyclical nature of business and management ideas is an empirical reality. Other aspects of these ideas, however, are typically matters of perspective. In the remainder of this chapter, we'll describe our own perspectives and philosophies of business ideas—informed, we believe, by the reality of life in organizations.

No Fads

The temporal rise and fall of business ideas in the press and in organizations leads to the temptation to classify them as fads, particularly as their life cycles become shorter and shorter. Previous books and articles have capitalized on an undercurrent of resentment about management ideas and a cynical suspicion that they're nothing at all but fads.[6] We, however, are more interested in the potential of these ideas to change organizations and to create true benefit. Yet it's still important to deal with the fad issue.

Business fads obviously don't follow the entire P cycle within organizations. Rather, they are short-lived states of enthusiasm that rarely deliver real benefit or change. Their effect on organizations is symbolized by the infamous acronym BOHICA, for "Bend over, here it comes again." Some organizations subject their managers and employees to a seemingly endless stream of new ideas, none of which ever really become fully implemented before the next one comes along. If you're more visual than verbal, glance at a few Dilbert cartoons, and you'll understand the syndrome well. If you prefer words, a quotation from Eileen Shapiro, a consultant friend of ours who has decried fad surfing, is indicative of the problem:

> *To review just a few of the options, you can, if you wish, flatten your pyramid, become a horizontal organization, and eliminate hierarchy from your company. You can empower your people, open your environment, and transform your culture. You can listen to your customers, create a customer-focused organization, and commit to total customer satisfaction. You can do the "vision thing," write a mission statement, and put together a strategic plan. You can improve continuously, shift your paradigms, and*

become a learning organization. You can devote yourself and your
company to total quality management. Or you can reengineer your
corporation. . . .[7]

By themselves, each of these ideas may be a perfectly reasonable thing to do. Doing them all at once—or doing any of them in
a shallow or vacuous manner—is the problem. In *Managing on the
Edge,* Richard Pascale does a particularly good job of making this
point. He decries the acceptance and utilization of ideas "without
an in-depth grasp of their underlying foundation, and without the
commitment necessary to sustain them."[8]

We don't question that some organizations have gotten carried
away with business fads. Of course, new business ideas can't substitute for the basics of management: hiring good people, using
resources wisely, and producing products and services of high
quality that customers want. Nor do we believe that it's a good
idea to blindly turn over your business to a guru or consultant
who professes to have seen the future—with your company not in
it. Skepticism and a "show me" attitude are perfectly appropriate
with these business nostrums.

But closing your mind to new ideas isn't desirable either. We
dare say that there's not a single management idea out there that
doesn't have some potential merit for some organizations. Certainly some ideas are better than others, and we'll help you distinguish a good idea from a bad one. Some ideas can be good for
others, but a poor fit to your organization at this time. But there's
a grain of value in almost every idea, and a bushel in some. Idea
practitioners should try to identify the useful components in
every idea they become aware of.

For example, we've never been fans of one of the ideas in
Shapiro's preceding quote: the horizontal organization. Although
we wish no offense to anyone who has promoted or adopted this
idea (some of whom are friends of ours), we consider it a little
bizarre to totally abandon all aspects of your organizational structure and hierarchy other than cross-functional business processes.
In fact, most managers realized that the horizontal organization

didn't make sense, and we've never seen a horizontal organization in anything like a pure form. But there is some hidden value in the horizontal organization notion. It's rhetoric that could lead a company to at least add a process dimension to its organizations. In its pure form, the idea could lead an organization down a dangerous path, but in a watered-down form, it could lead to substantial process improvements. Nobody needs a horizontal organization, but most organizations need to be more horizontal.

So what determines whether a business idea is faddish or something that can provide real value? We've concluded that the question is being asked incorrectly. It's not the idea itself that is faddish, but rather how the organization adopts it. In short, there are no faddish ideas—only faddish managers and companies. Some ideas are certainly more superficial and amenable to faddish pursuit than others, but that doesn't mean they are without potential merit.

Faddish organizations have the following attributes:

- They adopt new business ideas indiscriminately, without regard for fit to the organization.

- They treat new business ideas as panaceas that can solve all their problems.

- They drop all former idea-based initiatives in favor of a new one that comes along.

- They take up the most radical, outrageous formulation of the idea (employing apocalyptic and revolutionary rhetoric), rather than more conservative versions.

- They almost blindly follow someone's idea of the process for implementing an idea, without good evidence that it works or is worth pursuing.

- They talk about implementing an idea, but don't really supply sufficient resources or commitment to make anything happen.

- They (at least the leaders of the organization) don't personally involve themselves in the implementation of the idea, but rather turn it all over to outside consultants.

- They adopt more ideas than they can actually implement.

Perhaps obviously, the converse of each of these faddish approaches is the right way for organizations and individuals to get value out of emerging business and management ideas. That is, managers who know how to deal with ideas pay careful attention to the fit of the idea to the organization, rejecting those that are inappropriate. They minimize their expectations that any single new idea can change themselves or their organizations dramatically. They appreciate old and new ideas in combination. Their gurus are less radical and more reasoned. They don't turn over the implementation of new ideas to a consultant, but stay in charge of the change themselves. They supplement talk with action. And they place a firm limit on the amount and types of changes their organization can pursue. Such managers are truly wise practitioners of the art of new business and management ideas.

Nothing New Under the Sun

The motivating power of newness is familiar to anyone who has walked the aisles of a grocery store. Describing a managerial idea as new, fresh, and innovative will make it much more likely to get a hearing within your organization. One popular business magazine, *Business 2.0* (even the title suggests a new version), covers all the bases with its subtitle: *New Economy—New Rules— New Leaders*. But the idea of newness in business ideas is not itself new. The first issue of the *Harvard Business Review* in 1922 proclaimed, "In business, all things are new."[9]

The overwhelming majority of business ideas aren't entirely new. And even if they are, they may well be largely wrong! Every idea owes a considerable debt to related ideas that came before. And it's rare to encounter an idea that's so good and innovative that it should supplant related ones that came before it. The quality expert Bob Cole bemoaned the replacement of many organizations' quality programs with reengineering when the latter idea came along in the 1990s.[10] The organizations shouldn't have done this, because the two ideas addressed different objectives, both of which were valid. A more reasonable approach was to combine them: "In practice, most firms need to combine process improvement and process innovation [another term for reengineering] in an ongoing quality program. Ideally (though not necessarily), a company will attempt to stabilize a process and begin continuous improvement, then strive for process innovation. Lest it slide back down the slippery slope of process degradation, a firm should then pursue a program of continuous improvement for the post-innovation process. Furthermore, across an entire organization, innovation initiatives will be appropriate for some processes, continuous improvement initiatives for others."[11] In this case, an advocate of reengineering would first want to get the organization excited about the topic—calling it "new" if necessary to generate some enthusiasm—but then would try to work with advocates of other related or precursor ideas to reconcile them.

This tactic for reengineering suggests a broader approach. Idea practitioners should be aware that most business ideas have some relatively new components and some classical wisdom. It's up to the idea people to "decompose" the idea, or disaggregate it into its components, and to adopt the pieces—new or old—that make sense. For purposes of marketing the idea, it may sometimes be desirable to emphasize its novelty. Balancing the classical and fashionable aspects of business ideas requires that managers become much more aware of the rhetorical aspects of management ideas, the competitive and market environments, and the cultures and operations of their own organizations (discussed in chapters 5 and 6).

The current enthusiasm for customer relationship management (CRM), for example, might be broken down into the idea's basic components. Customer focus and getting to know the customer are both timeless ideas. The devotion of more attention to the best customers is an old idea now enabled with some new analytical technology. Finally, CRM includes some relatively new tools for increasing sales force productivity and knowledge sharing. The term "CRM" may then be a useful label for the adoption of some new capabilities and the reinforcement of some timeless philosophies also embodied in the idea.

Even "old" ideas can have remarkable power and relevance. For example, Barcy Fox, an idea practitioner who directs learning and training activities at the global executive search firm Russell Reynolds Associates (see sidebar), has worked for many years with companies—including her own employer—to try to change behaviors of employees in particular directions. She's a big believer in incentive compensation, having worked as a consultant in that field:

> *Rewarding people for the behaviors you want them to exhibit is hardly a new idea in business, but you'd be surprised by how many organizations still don't do it. They may offer increased compensation, but money is often among the worst motivators and the most expensive, particularly for getting changes in behavior or performance improvement. Incentive programs offering travel, training, or gifts from a catalog are generally much more effective and usually can be implemented for about one-third the cost of additional cash incentives. Leaders and managers frequently undervalue the impact of positive recognition for achievement: Many high achievers covet the recognition more than any other single form of reward. (Otherwise, you're just talking about the rules for awarding the bonuses. Those are the forms of gainsharing—cash, noncash—that's it.) Most importantly, you've got to make people feel that they are participating in the success—or the problems—of the organization.*

Fox reads widely and searches for new ideas all the time. But she also draws on time-honored principles of motivation and behavior change. Sometimes the best ideas are those that have been around for a while.

Barcy Fox, Idea Practitioner

Barcy Fox has been intellectually curious for her entire life. At college, she found it too constraining to have one major, so she simultaneously pursued English, philosophy, history, and art history. She might also have majored in organizational psychology, given her "intense interest in people and how to make the workplace better." One of her first jobs was at the ad agency Foote, Cone & Belding, where she learned the importance of communicating ideas effectively and getting the attention of people whose behavior needs to change. Fox then ended up at Maritz Inc., the company that pioneered incentive programs for salespeople. She had various jobs there during her seventeen years with the company, but one position seems ideal for an idea practitioner: product manager for the company's IdeaSystem service. This position involved setting up programs for 160-plus companies in which the employees could make suggestions and contribute ideas for cost reduction and performance improvement.

Fox learned two valuable lessons from that collection of projects. First, that ideas most often relate directly to the work that the employees actually do—work that they are experts at. Second, that there are two dominant forms of valuable creativity: genuine innovation, which everyone prizes, and "applied memory"—thinking mindfully and learning on the fly about how to apply what you know to new situations. The most important stimulus to applied memory is to create a "moment for noticing" by reminding people in positive, challenging ways to challenge the status quo.

At Russell Reynolds, her job is officially to lead learning and change programs, but her work goes well beyond filling seats in training programs. She's really focused on whatever it takes to achieve the behaviors her firm needs. Most recently, she has worked with the company's senior executives to try to increase the firm's focus on business development. In the boom years of the late 1990s, search firms had more business than they could handle. Today, however, to remain at the top of the global search business, Russell Reynolds will have to focus on generating business as well as filling client vacancies with great candidates. Helping to bring about that kind of idea-driven behavior change is Fox's specialty.

You Say You Want a Revolution

Newness is one way for business ideas to get attention; using revolutionary rhetoric is another. Our philosophy about revolutionary rhetoric in business ideas can be expressed as a paradox. That is, the ideas with the most power are often those couched in revolutionary terms. However, these are usually the worst ideas for a company to implement! They encourage organizations to take on the most problematic formulations of the idea and to raise expectations well beyond attainable results. How can organizations deal with this dilemma?

Business book authors and journalists well understand that wrapping an idea in earth-shattering rhetoric is a way to get attention. This rhetoric is therefore a common technique in business books and magazines, whose covers are adorned with such phrases as "Everything you know about business is wrong!" "The Internet changes everything," "The end of progress!" and every conceivable usage of the word "revolution." The trusting manager who reads and believes these sources would be wide-eyed indeed.

Boastful rhetoric aside, it would be quite difficult to come up with a truly revolutionary business idea. As we've noted, most of these business ideas are riffs on a few basic themes—innovation, efficiency, effectiveness, and so forth. When business gurus talk about revolution, they're usually advocating innovation. This sort of advocacy is nothing new. Some management scholars have pointed out, however, that gurus of the first half of the twentieth century were much more likely to acknowledge classic themes than were those of the second half of the century—even though the later generation was still writing and speaking about these themes. Perhaps with the proliferation of management ideas and gurus, the need to differentiate themselves from each other and from those coming before them has become more pronounced.[12]

We'd even argue that the virtues of revolution are overrated. Revolutions are necessary when companies have fallen behind their competitors or when they have become very lax in key processes. But the best companies never have to resort to revolution. As Peter Brabeck, CEO of Nestlé, put it, "Big, dramatic change is fine for a crisis. If you come in as CEO and a turnaround is necessary, then fine, have a revolution. . . . But not every company is in crisis all the time. Many companies are like us—not as big, of course—but they are performing well. Growing, innovating, and so forth—good and fit. Why should we manufacture dramatic change? Just for change's sake? To follow some sort of fad without logical thinking behind it? . . . You can have slow and steady change, and that is nothing to be ashamed of."[13]

How do idea-oriented managers deal with this contradiction— that revolutionary rhetoric gets attention, but may be harmful in the long run? Again the answer is that managers should be conscious of the paradox, but not overly cynical about it. Some dramatically different challenges seem to come along every few decades (e.g., globalization, the Internet, and the service economy). Big ideas certainly form around these developments, though they usually take a long time to come to fruition. Managers who want to import these ideas into their own organizations can emphasize their revolutionary potential in the beginning, but should make their organizations aware that implementation is likely to be evolutionary and to involve some classical issues around organizational change and inertia. They should perhaps seek out the more revolutionary formulations of new business ideas to get their colleagues excited, create energy, and motivate the organization to pursue the idea, but they should find calmer-headed versions of the idea to guide its implementation.

There is no simple answer to the problem of balancing rhetoric and reality in the management of new business ideas. Those who bring ideas into organizations have to walk a fine line. They must balance new ideas with old ones, and radical ideas with conservative ones. They must extract what is truly new and useful from ideas that will also contain tried-and-true messages. They must use rhetoric to their advantage, but be wary of exploiting it or raising expectations too far with it.

The Importance of Perspective

An executive we interviewed told us about an issue that had been bothering him for some time. He works for a benefits outsourcing firm, one of the largest in the world, and was now formally responsible for introducing and sponsoring ideas around this global organization. He had an aptitude for ideas, was discerning, and knew why he believed in some more than others. But there still was something missing in his overall approach to ideas. He just could not pin down exactly what it was, he explained.

> Then, last week, I was in a training session with senior managers and other executives. One of the trainers walked up to the white board and drew a picture of three linked circles to explain the best way to communicate with employees. The first read "Science," the second "Art," the third "Reality." Art had to do with various conversational styles; science had to do with formalized policies, procedures, and prescribed terminologies. Reality, he told us, is the situation you're applying it to. I looked at that and I thought, "Oh my God, that's what I'm missing: the ability to bring multiple points of view to bear when looking at ideas." I don't want to sound melodramatic, but this was an important flash of insight.

Those who consistently apply multiple points of view will almost invariably be more successful in social or intellectual endeavors than those who—on account of obstinacy or ignorance—apply just one. The best negotiators, political leaders, and researchers do it all the time. To prove guilt, a top district attorney will apply the points of view of DNA science to show links to physical evidence, common sense to establish motive, and sense of timing to establish opportunity.

As discussed, some of the most effective points of view when it comes to thinking about business ideas are also somewhat paradoxical. The successful idea practitioner will be able to keep both sides in mind at once. The first point of view relates to the life cycles described earlier in this chapter. As described, the most important perspective is to know just what constitutes success inside the idea practitioner's organization, and the idea's current status with regard to those criteria. At the same time, the idea-oriented executive needs to be aware of where the idea stands in the external marketplace of business notions. The idea shouldn't be adopted because it's popular, but there's nothing wrong with taking advantage of the popularity of a good and appropriate idea.

A second point of view might be called "skeptical optimism" and relates to the faddish nature of management ideas. We've explained that there are no totally bad ideas—though some come close! This optimistic view will encourage idea practitioners to seek out the valuable nuggets in ideas they hear about. At the same time, a good idea practitioner remains a bit skeptical that any idea is so brilliant and insightful that it could solve all an organization's problems.

The final paradoxical attribute of the idea practitioner is a "radical conservative" view of management ideas. Such an individual would realize that new and radical ideas have rhetorical power, but would use the power conservatively. New and revolutionary formulations of ideas may get the attention of the organization, but may also raise expectations beyond what is possible. The capable idea practitioner uses rhetoric with care and precision.

Ideas and Implementation

Despite the importance of ideas, we need to keep them in perspective. Ideas themselves are the sexier part of making business change happen. The intellectual stimulation the ideas provide draws not only idea practitioners, but also the press, consultants, researchers, and other groups. But ideas are also the easy part. It's relatively straightforward to select and understand a management idea, but quite difficult to do all the other things an idea practitioner needs to do: communicate the idea to others, persuade them of its merits, overcome politics and inertia, get a pilot going, enlist executive support, measure progress, and so on.

We're not disparaging the importance of ideas; they are for us the most interesting aspect of business change. Change without ideas is likely to fail and is certainly likely to be boring. But ideas without implementation don't yield much value either; intellectual stimulation is not business value.

Chapter 2 and this one have covered idea practitioners and the ideas they employ. These are two key resources in bringing about idea-driven change. The other key resource is the guru—the individual who makes a living from business ideas. Business gurus are the topic of chapter 4.

4

THE GUIDE TO GURUS

WHERE GOOD MANAGEMENT
IDEAS COME FROM

IF IDEA PRACTITIONERS are the ringleaders of idea-based change, what's the role of business gurus? And don't gurus already receive more attention than they deserve? Perhaps, but even in our practitioner-centric view, there's still an important role for gurus. Gurus don't necessarily create business and management ideas from scratch, but they certainly help package and broadcast them. An idea practitioner who wishes to be effective at managing ideas should be well acquainted with the most prominent and productive business thinkers. Just as any customer should be knowledgeable about and have good relationships with key suppliers and distributors, idea practitioners should know both the individual gurus and the processes by which they work.

Of course, business ideas are available in books, magazines, and newspapers. But ideas come from people, not disembodied sources. New movements in business and elsewhere need a guru to propagate the idea—to spread throughout the land the tales of the power and potential of the new approach. Gurus pull ideas out of the air and give them structure; business movements lacking a guru never get very far. Gurus give the ideas not only a face, but also a blessing and the evangelism needed to convert skeptical businesspeople to the new faith. Like the original, religious gurus of central Asia, our business gurus have ties to "magic." That is, they are charismatic, appear somewhat mysterious, and employ methods that are only vaguely understood. And while they are respected and admired, they are also (particularly in the pragmatic United States) suspected of purveying worthless nostrums and fads.

Religious gurus have been found throughout human history, but business gurus go back only about a century. Frederick Winslow Taylor, whose ideas became popular in the early twentieth century, was probably the first business guru, preaching the gospel of efficiency, process improvement, and time-and-motion studies. Although these ideas seem highly rational, Taylor was not without messianic fervor for his notion of scientific management:

> No system of management, no single expedient within the control of any man or any set of men can insure continuous prosperity to either workmen or employers. Prosperity depends upon so many factors entirely beyond the control of any one set of men, any state, or even any one country, that certain periods will inevitably come when both sides must suffer, more or less. It is claimed, however, that under scientific management the intermediate periods will be far more prosperous, far happier, and more free from discord and dissension. And also, that the periods will be fewer, shorter and the suffering less. And this will be particularly true in any one town, any one section of the country, or any one state which first substitutes the principles of scientific management for the rule of thumb.[1]

Of course, not all gurus are alike. Some, like Taylor, doggedly advocate one idea throughout their careers as gurus. In modern times, Michael Hammer has single-mindedly advocated business process reengineering; in earlier years, W. Edwards Deming never abandoned the ideals of quality and statistical process control. Other gurus, such as Tom Peters and Gary Hamel, jump from one related topic to another. Some gurus—we might call them über-gurus—essentially become their own movement, as did Peter Drucker, or to a lesser degree, Charles Handy in the United Kingdom. They feel able to pronounce upon almost any topic, and their devotees can be said to worship at the altar of the guru himself or herself more than any specific idea.

What Role Do Gurus Play in Business Idea Creation?

In describing the role gurus play in business ideas, "create" isn't exactly the right word. Gurus tend to assemble, package, and broadcast business ideas; they will rarely create the whole thing from scratch. As discussed in chapter 3, most "new" business ideas have been seen in some form before. What the gurus do is to take the components of an idea, reshuffle them a bit, add some description and some examples, package them up as an appealing concept, and publish and present them.

As an illustration, let's take the idea of core competence that surfaced in the 1990s as an approach to business strategy. The idea suggests that firms should identify some activity at which they already excel or could plausibly excel in the future, and make that the centerpiece of their strategy. This idea was most recently advanced by Gary Hamel and C. K. Prahalad in a 1990 *Harvard Business Review* article, "The Core Competence of the Corporation."[2]

Was this idea new? Not particularly. Academics had talked for decades about the "resource-based view of the firm." Edith Penrose, for example, published *The Theory of the Firm,* generally considered the first book with a resource-based perspective, in 1956.[3] The theory suggested that firms should stick to the activities at which they are internally competent. Most businesspeople would hardly be shocked at the idea of identifying some activity at which you are competent and building your business around that.

So what did Hamel and Prahalad bring to the table? Both gurus are clearly smart and highly knowledgeable about business and have a good sense of timing. They rounded up some nice contemporary examples of core competence, including NEC's semiconductors, Canon's microelectronics, and Honda's small engine design. Note that all of these examples are Japanese companies, though several non-Japanese firms are also mentioned in the article. When the 1990 article was published, Japan's economy was performing well, and Western managers were anxious to learn the secrets of their success. Hamel and Prahalad combined the old resource-based view with the emphasis on differentiation made popular in the 1980s by Michael Porter. In general, these gurus made academic concepts readable for a managerial audience. And they wrapped it all in an attractive, alliterative title.

Hamel and Prahalad are leading strategy gurus, and their success isn't based only on the core competence ideas. But their other notions—strategy as revolution, strategy as stretch and leverage, competing for the future—have similar attributes to the competence idea. They are plausible, stated in an interesting manner, and wrapped in compelling rhetoric. Rich stories are presented to validate the concepts. It may seem as if we are disparaging their work, but we're not: Their work is among the best of usable business strategy research and writing, and we'd be flattered if our own work were compared to theirs.

In fact, it's important for gurus not to disparage others' ideas. In light of our argument that there are no useless business ideas, gurus do the business world a disservice by broadly criticizing ideas not of their own making. In Gary Hamel's most recent book, *Leading the Revolution,* for example, he takes aim at continuous improvement, reengineering, enterprise resource planning, organizational learning, and knowledge management. He describes these ideas as linear, whereas his own nostrums are, of course, nonlinear: "In a nonlinear world, only nonlinear ideas will create new wealth."[4] Of course, the book came out at the height of the dot-com frenzy; perhaps linear ideas have a little more value in Hamel's mind today.

What Are the General Attributes of Gurus?

In addition to the need to set themselves apart, gurus have other traits in common. Like the idea practitioners they work with in companies, gurus tend to be boundary spanners. Their exposure to both theory and practice-oriented ideas makes them uniquely suited to develop new business ideas. Although we'll later discuss some important differences in their backgrounds, their daily activities tend to be similar and to cut across categories. Consultants may teach and often manage their own firms; business-oriented professors may well do consulting and even occasionally become managers. CEOs may become consultants or teachers when they retire. Almost all gurus do some research, some writing, some speaking, and some consulting.

The great paradox of these individuals is that they may often be extremely successful in financial terms and have high status with the public, but they are typically somewhat marginal within their own professions. The most popular business academics, for example, are frequently disparaged by their professorial colleagues for having "sold out" or for doing work that is too relevant and not sufficiently rigorous. Consultants who devote their days to "thought leadership" don't necessarily get the same status or rewards as those who sell big consulting projects. Managers who write books and hit the lecture circuit may be disparaged by those within their firms who feel they aren't minding the store. These people may be envied by many outside observers, but not necessarily by their own colleagues!

Gurus may appear to be individual geniuses, but they seldom work alone. Business professors rely on graduate students and junior professors to help with their research; senior consultants stand on the shoulders of junior ones. Sometimes, ideas actually developed by a junior or middle-level executive become identified with a firm's senior leadership. And all gurus benefit from the ideas of their book and journal editors. We'll describe the group-based nature of managerial innovation with respect to reengineering and knowledge management in later chapters. Gurus with a high degree of integrity give credit to their teams. For example, in his book *Good to Great,* Jim Collins not only thanks his research team but includes a picture of it in the book.

Ideas may even move from middle management (most likely, an idea practitioner) to a guru from another background. The idea of the balanced scorecard, for example, is closely identified with academic Robert Kaplan and consultant David Norton. But the first balanced scorecard was created in the mid-1980s by a midlevel quality manager named Art Schneiderman (now an independent consultant) at Analog Devices.[5] Kaplan discovered the innovative work in the course of visiting Analog and writing a Harvard case study about the company. Norton headed a consulting firm that studied Analog's experiences in the context of a multiclient research program. Both Kaplan and Norton have done a great deal to refine and popularize the balanced scorecard idea, but they didn't create it.

Although gurus vary in how they go about their work, all of them must do three things: interact with companies, think and write, and present their ideas at meetings and conferences. Gurus don't succeed unless they are good at communicating in all these contexts.

First, they need to interact with companies because that's typically the primary source of their ideas. They may encounter the companies in consulting projects, research, or managerial experience. As one guru put it in an academic study of the role of gurus: "Of course I have been influenced by other people's research. But I find that if I want to know what's going on, what's happening out there, I need to speak to managers. And this is what I do. I speak to thousands of managers every year. What they tell me helps to structure my ideas. Trying ideas out on them and seeing their response, hearing their views, helps me to choose those ideas that seem most relevant and are more likely to work. I do not claim to have original ideas. Rather I am a translator and popularizer of ideas."[6]

Several important business ideas of the 1990s were created or refined in a vehicle specifically designed for creating contact between researchers/consultants and companies: the so-called multiclient research program. These projects, typically offered by consulting firms but occasionally by business schools, gather together a number of companies that were willing to pay (typically a few tens of thousands of dollars) to jointly explore a particular topic. In the 1990s, such topics as agility, the balanced scorecard, value disciplines, disruptive technologies, and reengineering and knowledge management (discussed in later chapters) were significantly shaped by multiclient research programs. The proliferation of these multiparty programs suggests that new business ideas spring more from the interactions of gurus with business practice and idea practitioners than from the mind of the guru alone.

Even gurus who do not have journalistic backgrounds can be viewed as sophisticated journalists: they see or hear about someone doing something interesting, interpret it within a broader context, and then chronicle it for others. The organization that's doing the leading practice may not even be aware of what it's doing, or may not have described the practice in an appealing way—that's the role of the guru. In many cases, the successful guru is in close contact with the company's idea practitioners whom we described in chapter 3.

Gurus have to write—books, journal articles, magazine columns, book reviews, white papers, online content, and every other form of business literature. Fortunately for the gurus, the 1990s saw an enormous growth in the number of business books and magazines, and the advent of hundreds of Web sites offering business content. Unfortunately for these individuals, with so much text out there, it becomes harder and harder for any person to get the attention of the business audience. It used to be, for example, that a couple of articles in the *Harvard Business Review* practically guaranteed guruhood. Now, however, it's only a beginning.

But writing alone isn't enough. Any guru wanting to be in the major leagues has to hit the road for conferences and corporate speaking engagements. In a good year, more than ten thousand business conferences, workshops, trade shows, meetings, and other events are scheduled—and every one of them needs content.[7] Gurus benefit greatly by speaking at these conferences, not only in getting their messages out to the world, but also in generating extra income. The most successful gurus can earn forty thousand dollars or more for a one-hour speech. Unfortunately, we don't generally fall into that category, so call us if you want a bargain.

Ranking Business Gurus

As mentioned, gurus need to be visible—to write and be written about, to speak and be spoken about—to have impact. The advent of the World Wide Web and of various online databases enable the objective evaluation of the impact of a number of business gurus. Appendix C ranks the top two hundred business gurus. We started from an even larger list of more than three hundred, ranking them by three criteria used by federal judge Richard Posner to create a similar list of "public intellectuals":

- hits on the Internet search engine Google using the various forms of a guru's name, minus any hits not related to the guru

- citations in the Social Sciences Citation Index—that is, the number of times that academics have cited the guru's published work

- media mentions in the LexisNexis online database of business and popular media[8]

The combined ranking is based on the sum of ranks on each of the three criteria.[9]

The combination of these criteria produces an interesting—and respectable—list, in our opinion better than any of the subjective lists we've seen elsewhere. The top ten names are more or less what one would expect to find:

1. **Michael Porter:** a very well-known strategist who teaches at Harvard Business School, and author of two seminal works of strategy, *Competitive Strategy* and *Competitive Advantage*

2. **Tom Peters:** the hyper-energetic writer and speaker, co-author of *In Search of Excellence,* and author of many other best-selling books

3. **Robert Reich:** author of *The Future of Success* and *The Work of Nations* and secretary of labor in the Clinton administration

4. **Peter Drucker:** the world's most prominent management guru for decades and professor at Claremont Graduate School

5. **Gary Becker:** University of Chicago labor social economist, *Business Week* columnist, and Nobel Prize winner

6. **Peter Senge:** MIT researcher on organizational learning and author of the best-selling *The Fifth Discipline*

7. **Gary Hamel:** strategist and author of *Leading the Revolution*

8. **Alvin Toffler:** best-selling author of business and social commentary such as *Future Shock*

9. **Hal Varian:** dean of the University of California, Berkeley School of Information Management Studies and author of *Information Rules*

10. **Dan Goleman:** social psychologist and author of several books on emotional intelligence and leadership

Each of these gurus has a niche in the world of business, one or more big books, and a means of receiving continual media attention. Some of those gurus at the top of the list are relative newcomers (Goleman and Reich, for example). Others, such as Drucker and Toffler, have been in the guru business for decades. Most of these names are serious business thinkers; only a few of the top two hundred would be considered lightweights by most observers. A few CEOs even managed to overcome the hurdle of academic citations to make it into the top two hundred, but then they probably have distinct advantages in media mentions and Web hits, since they control large communications and public-relations staffs. Newspaper and magazine columnists (e.g., Peters, Becker, and Varian) and Nobel Prize winners (Becker, Merton, and Scholes) do well in the rankings, for obvious reasons.

What is most striking about the list is the paucity of women (only six in the top one hundred—Rosabeth Moss Kanter, Esther Dyson, Patty Seybold, Martha Rogers, Meg Wheatley, and Kathleen Eisenhardt) and non-U.S. residents (eight in the top hundred—Charles Handy, Don Tapscott, Edward DeBono, Ken Ohmae, Sumantra Ghoshal, Richard Branson, Jiro Nonaka, and Geert Hofstede). The American business hype machine, which sets the world standard, clearly favors its own.

Managers with a strong interest in business gurus can peruse the list and find the thinkers who are most influential in their own management beliefs. The most ardent pursuers of business ideas may want to use Google to explore business gurus with whom they are unfamiliar.

Backgrounds of Business Gurus

These mysterious and charismatic individuals can come from a variety of backgrounds. And the backgrounds can make a difference in the nature and quality of the ideas. Advice about management from gurus with professorial backgrounds, for example, is likely to be somewhat different from that given by consultants or experienced managers who have become gurus.

Which of these sources might yield the best ideas, with the least effort in unproductive searching? It's important to know where to look for management ideas, and where not to look. Idea practitioners can waste a lot of time, money, and effort looking in the wrong places for innovative and useful business improvement approaches. Some potential sources of these ideas have built-in problems and flaws, yielding business ideas that aren't that good or particularly useful.

And even when the ideas are of high quality, a manager may need to take into account any built-in biases or contextual factors before applying the ideas. New business approaches from consultants, for example, may be designed to sell consulting projects; ideas from respected academics may be rigorous and empirically tested, but narrow. There are, of course, exceptions to the general rules we offer on sources. Consequently, even after deciding on a preferred source, any manager should keep his or her eyes open to ensure that important ideas aren't missed.

In the remainder of this chapter, we'll describe the strengths, weaknesses, and other attributes of gurus in terms of the following four most common backgrounds of business gurus:

- **Business Academics:** Business school faculty can undertake research and writing that is relevant to managers. Academics not only conduct research and teach, but usually do consulting and speaking on the side. Examples of this class include Michael Porter at Harvard, C. K. Prahalad at the University of Michigan, and Lester Thurow at MIT.

- **Consultants:** These people primarily work for consulting firms, though at least one of their primary roles involves generating thought leadership. In that capacity, they write articles and books and speak at conferences and individual companies. Examples include Adrian Slywotzky at Mercer

Management Consulting, Jim Champy at Perot Systems, and Lowell Bryan at McKinsey & Company.

- **Practicing Managers:** Usually CEOs of large, successful companies, these people write or speak on the management approaches their firms have adopted. Prominent examples include the ubiquitous Jack Welch of General Electric, Andy Grove of Intel, and among smaller firms, Jack Stack of Springfield ReManufacturing.

- **Journalists:** These people are writers or editors from business magazines or newspapers; they also write books. Examples of this class of idea producers include Tom Stewart at *Harvard Business Review* and formerly *Fortune* and *Business 2.0* (and author of *Intellectual Capital*), John Byrne at *Business Week* (and author of *The Whiz Kids* and coauthor of *Jack: Straight from the Gut*), and Adrian Wooldridge and John Micklethwait at *The Economist* (and authors of *A Future Perfect* and *The Witch Doctors*).

As we've mentioned, gurus often cross boundaries. And a few business gurus may now be nothing but gurus—they are no longer affiliated with any institution but themselves. But for most individuals, their primary current or previous role falls into one on the preceding list. Often, the best way to categorize a guru's background is to look at the source of his or her income. We'd have to label ourselves consultants, for example, since our bread is primarily buttered by consulting firms.

Business Academics as Gurus

Business school professors would seem to be the ideal role for creating and disseminating business ideas. After all, professors are almost always smart and have few responsibilities in their jobs beyond teaching and writing (OK, there are also lots of committee meetings—one key reason why we aren't full-time academics). Their students can easily function as sounding boards (or guinea pigs) for the testing of emerging ideas. And if the mission of business schools isn't the creation and dissemination of useful business ideas, what is it?

Good question. If that is the mission of business schools, then they don't perform it very well. We believe that most business schools—and most academics who inhabit them—have not been very effective in the creation of *useful* business ideas. Sure, a lot of business ideas are explored in business school research, but for the most part, they are created elsewhere and are seldom even discussed in an accessible fashion by academics.

Sadly, academics are almost always rewarded for rigor over relevance in their research. They get more credit, and are more likely to be promoted and tenured, for writing narrow, highly quantitative, and difficult-to-understand academic papers in obscure journals than they do for producing blockbuster business ideas. Most business school academics simply don't know much about real businesses, because they don't have much contact with them. As Bob Sutton, a Stanford University professor who does work with real businesses, put it: "Most management scholars spend their time 'studying' organizations and life within them by analyzing archived statistical evidence on computers, doing contrived experiments with undergraduates or M.B.A.'s, or writing 'theory' that is based in pure logic that is unsullied by actual evidence. In other words, many of these scholars rarely—if ever—venture into the real worlds they claim to be expert about.[10]

Besides Sutton, there are other exceptions to the academics-make-poor-gurus rule, of course. We've already mentioned some of them—and later we'll describe a very prominent exception. For the most part, however, the realm of business academia is a wasteland for the practicing manager.

How did this unfortunate disconnect between academics and business come about? The first business schools, founded in the beginning of the twentieth century, didn't always major in irrelevance. Early business researcher Elton Mayo, for example, discovered the famous "Hawthorne effect"—that workers' productivity

was based in part on whether they felt their managers were pay-
ing attention to them—in a study of Western Electric employees.

In the 1950s, however, the Ford and Carnegie foundations issued reports arguing that business schools were lacking in rigor
and needed a substantial injection of social science if they were
to become intellectually respectable. With the aid of money from
these foundations, business schools began to hire substantial
numbers of Ph.D. psychologists, sociologists, and particularly
economists. These academics cared less about the application of
their ideas to business practice and more about how other academics viewed their work. The preferred outlets for publication
shifted from the *Harvard Business Review*—viewed as insuffi-
ciently rigorous and overly relevant (it was listed as a "trade journal" in one top-twenty business school's list of places its faculty
published)—to *Administrative Science Quarterly (ASQ)* and *Management Science*. These publications may be high in scholarly
rigor, but they are virtually impenetrable by the average manager. Even the abstracts of the articles—intended to be a relatively simple description—are difficult to understand; one issue
of *ASQ* featured these lines from the abstract of one article (and
such language is not at all uncommon): "The organizations in-
voked coercive and mimetic pressures to account for and justify
the new structure, and they associated the innovation with le-
gitimated organizational activities. The findings make two contributions that link the 'old' institutionalism and neoinstitutional-
ism: they point to organizational agency in the preventive use of
the very institutional forces that create isomorphism and suggest
the presence of institutional forces even during the early stages of
innovation."[11]

Not surprisingly, *ASQ* is poorly read—or more likely, not read
at all—by managers. It has a circulation of less than five thousand
subscriptions, almost all of which go to academics or libraries.

Even Harvard Business School, historically the bastion of research relevant to managers, has shifted its focus toward some
version of rigor. As one professor put it, "This place has been over-

run in the past several years by highly academic economists." One junior faculty member concluded that at Harvard, professors must master both the rigor and the relevance objectives to receive promotion and tenure. "I felt like I had to publish in both *HBR* and *ASQ*," he said. "I did it for a few years, but I didn't really like the *ASQ*-style work." Although this professor did publish both types of work successfully for a few years, he ultimately left Harvard for a consulting firm, where he hoped to focus on managerially relevant research.

Our shining example of an academic as guru is Warren Bennis (twentieth on our list in appendix C). We have a lot of respect for this man, who has written twenty-eight books and most of the leading tomes on leadership—including *On Becoming a Leader* and *Geeks and Geezers: Leadership Across the Generations*.[12] He's also a near-octogenarian with a mind as sharp as a switchblade and a manner as polished as marble. So we were surprised to hear him say that he too felt like a somewhat marginal character in the world of business academia: "At USC [University of Southern California, where he is a professor] there is a skewed emphasis on 'top-tier' academic journals. I read none of them, and most people in my position don't. Hardly any faculty other than myself at USC are concerned with the practitioner stakeholder. I'm viewed as a colorful, exotic animal that they wheel out on special occasions—a marquee person. But hardly mainstream. No doctoral students, for example, have ever asked me to chair their committees—it wouldn't be good for their careers."

Bennis was a conventional business academic in his early years, publishing in academic sociology journals and in equally academic journals of organizational behavior. As an assistant professor at MIT and Boston University, he was headed toward a brilliant, if somewhat irrelevant, career as an academic. Yet somehow he concluded that he should explore academic administration, becoming provost of the State University of New York at Buffalo and then president of the University of Cincinnati. It is rare for organizational behavior scholars to actually try practicing what they preach! When he returned to the professorial life in the early 1980s, he was no longer content with writing scholarly papers on esoteric topics. Bennis became the rarest of boundary spanners: the writer on leadership who had actually been a leader. He also illustrates the social nature of "gurudom": Having had many collaborators over the years, Bennis always acknowledges their contributions.

Bennis has been around academia long enough to notice a change in the way business schools work. When he first became an academic in the late 1950s, the emphasis was more on applied tools and the value of experience. In 1959, he notes, "Managers from the Framingham General Motors plant taught production at MIT. Five years later, the focus of the class was linear programming, and their insights were deemed no longer appropriate." Bennis cites the 1959 Ford and Carnegie foundation reports as being a turning point in business schools. On the one hand, they injected a needed dose of rigor. On the other hand, many programs became rigorous to the point of irrelevance. He feels that thought leaders in other fields such as consulting and journalism have developed primarily in response to the vacuum created by business schools. In his view, the emphasis on rigor is currently at a peak, but he believes that it will subside: "There is no other professional field in which practitioners are so disconnected from their professional schools. In architecture, for an advanced degree you work with a faculty member to design a building. In medicine, each medical student works with a faculty member to begin treating a family. Business schools will eventually take more seriously the need for creating reflective business practitioners." We hope that he is right.

Consultants as Gurus

Management consultants have become some of the most prolific idea creators in the 1980s and 1990s. They were heavily involved in new strategy ideas (e.g., the famous Boston Consulting Group growth-share matrix, with its dogs, cash cows, and stars), reengineering, value disciplines, knowledge management, profit pools, and so on. For consultants, the appeal of generating business ideas is that they can help to implement those ideas in their clients' businesses. This innovation can be profitable for both parties. For example, business process reengineering, which improved many companies' processes, largely emerged from consulting firms, and it became a major practice area for them. As a result of this appeal, several consulting firms—including ours—have created extensive research centers or think tanks to lead the development of new business ideas.

Despite their reputations as purveyors of new business ideas, not all consultants are gurus. Many firms sell services that are not particularly innovative or conceptual. Even within innovative firms, the majority of consultants sell and deliver ideas created by others. Only a relatively small percentage of individuals who call themselves management consultants have ever written an article or a book.

Consultants who do desire to become gurus, however, have a number of potential strengths in business idea creation. Even the average management consultant at many firms will have an M.B.A. from a leading business school; those who work in consulting R&D groups are often former business school professors with Ph.D.'s. Consultants visit and work with a wide variety of firms that can serve as research sites. Since they make money by solving real-world business problems, the research that emerges from them is likely to be relevant to managers and grounded in practice.

Consultants also have some constraints as gurus, however. The most important may be that the typical consultant doesn't have time to conduct research and produce articles and books. He or she is too busy serving clients and making money to become a guru. The rare consultant can use client engagements as fodder for research, and write on airplanes. Some firms, such as McKinsey, strongly encourage consultants to publish articles and take on the guru mantle. In others, it is tolerated at best.

Another constraint is that consultants may create or use the ideas primarily for marketing purposes. The research itself may be tainted by the desire to use the ideas to sell work; not all consulting-based research is self-serving, but some of it is. Like academic research, consultant research can also be jargon-filled and difficult to understand. Consultants may be too busy to conduct rigorous research and publish articles; some may be guilty of producing "PowerPoint-based" decks, with little rigor or evidence. Finally, in their zeal to market ideas, consultants may sometimes cross the line into inappropriate business practices. It's pretty clear, for example, that some CSC Index consultants or affiliates inappropriately manipulated the *New York Times* best-selling book list to ensure that their book (*The Discipline of Market Leaders*) made the list. They found out which bookstores reported their sales to the *Times* and then orchestrated a pattern of purchases at those stores to ensure a ranking as a best-seller. That ranking, of course, meant even more book sales and much higher visibility.

One consultant whose ideas are not intended to be self-serving is Fred Reichheld of Bain & Company (tied for seventy-third on our list). Reichheld is a passionate believer in the value of loyalty in business. His books *The Loyalty Effect* and *Loyalty Rules!* describe how companies that practice loyalty-based management—to customers, employees, and shareholders—outperform their competitors.[13] In addition to practicing the principles of loyalty in his own personal life Reichheld also believes that Bain is much more loyalty oriented than other consulting firms.

Reichheld's role at Bain, however, illustrates some of the difficulties that practicing consultants face when attempting to become experts or gurus. He wrote his first book while leading Bain's consulting practice on loyalty management. He then decided, however, that it was too difficult to do research, write, and speak while remaining a full-time consultant. Reichheld was able to persuade Bain's leaders to create a new half-time role called Bain Fellow. The job allowed him to produce a second book, to write several articles for the *Harvard Business Review*, to organize seminars for CEOs who believe in and practice loyalty management, and to speak frequently to audiences on the topic. Like thought leaders with other backgrounds, Reichheld assumes a role that takes him out of the managerial hierarchy of Bain. He nevertheless maintains a mutually beneficial relationship with Bain—a relationship consistent with his personal priorities and true to the principles of loyalty. The Bain Fellow position will accommodate other senior Bain partners who choose to focus in the arena of intellectual leadership.

There is another type of consultant, which we'll label the academic refugee. These individuals have attributes of both the consultant and the academic. They were academics at an early stage in their careers, but they no longer bother much with undergraduate or M.B.A. teaching or committee work. Instead, they've developed organizations—typically quite small—focused around their own reputations. These academic refugees give presentations to executives, do some high-profile consulting engagements, and write books and articles. Examples of this category of consultant include Stan Davis, Gary Hamel, Michael Hammer, and Geoffrey Moore.

Jim Collins, author of the best-selling *Good to Great* and tied for seventieth on our list, is another example of a former academic who now runs his own show. As an academic at Stanford Business School, Collins won teaching awards and collaborated with Jerry Porras on the highly successful book *Built to Last*. But he felt that his work wasn't being advanced by the academic environment: "The work Jerry Porras and I did on *Built to Last* did not fit squarely into the type of research generally favored at Stanford. I've often said, only partly tongue in cheek, that we succeeded largely in spite of Stanford, not because of Stanford. The late John Gardner challenged me to not fall into the trap of 'answering questions of increasing irrelevance with increasing precision.' So, I decided to become an entrepreneurial professor, rather than a professor of entrepreneurship. I formed my own management research laboratory, where I could work on big-scale research projects on whatever topics interested me. In effect, I became a self-employed professor, endowed my own chair, and granted myself tenure." Perhaps other gurus should form similar institutions!

Practicing Managers as Gurus

Since Alfred P. Sloan published *My Years with General Motors* in 1963, it has become common for CEOs to describe the accomplishments of the companies they led in books, articles, and speeches. Lee Iacocca of Chrysler, Sam Walton of Wal-Mart, and Ray Kroc of McDonald's are only a few of the many examples of this phenomenon. Indeed, in the United States, there supposedly exists a "cult of the CEO," endowing the holders of that position with more positive traits—including idea creation—than they may deserve.

The idea that active managers themselves can be the source of influential ideas is far from new; it dates back at least to the 1930s. Chester Barnard, the president of New Jersey Bell, one of the old AT&T local units, was an unusually reflective man. He kept diaries and notes on his own and his fellow executives' activities, and in 1938 put together his thoughts in the authoritatively titled *The Functions of the Executive,* published by the equally authoritative Harvard University Press. Charles Perrow, a Yale professor of organizational studies, describes one of the contributions of this book: "This enormously influential and remarkable book contains within it three distinct trends of organizational theory that were to dominate the field for the next three decades."[14] The three fields Perrow mentions are human resource management, decision making, and institutional development. Perrow goes further and equates Barnard's influence with the great sociologist Max Weber!

Barnard's ideas permeated and dominated business school thinking until near the end of the twentieth century, although probably few current M.B.A.'s or executives under fifty would recognize his name or his influence. Barnard was one of the first executive practitioners to theorize about organizations in a systematic and academic manner. He emphasized just how organizations themselves were best understood as systems, and how strongly their success depended on what we might today call their social capital, that is, trust, informal networks, and social norms.[15]

As CEO of General Motors, Alfred Sloan was just as influential as Barnard, and much more visible. Many consider his magnum opus, *My Years with General Motors,* a masterpiece in the growing literature of "CEO as master strategist." Sloan took General Motors from a poorly performing and badly coordinated collection of semiautonomous units and helped (and he did have help!) develop the multidivision structure and strategies far better suited for increasing productivity in a huge, complex organization such as GM. Chris Bartlett and Sumantra Ghoshal describe the almost mythical image of Sloan: "The powerful, even heroic image of the CEO as omniscient strategist has been ingrained in business history and elaborated through management folklore. Few of today's practitioners have escaped hearing how Sloan conceived of the classic five-tiered product-market segmentation strategy that powered General Motors for over the first half of the century."[16]

Sloan's influence is still prevalent. His reputation has been further burnished by Peter Drucker (whom he hired as a consultant) and the influential business historian Alfred Chandler, and his is still a strong presence in most books and theories focusing on structure/strategy fit. Even Bill Gates reputedly believes that *My Years with General Motors* is the most important business book one can read!

As we've suggested in Sloan's case, CEOs are subject to one of the slightly deflating attributes noted with respect to gurus: They don't develop all the ideas by themselves. It's only natural that a large company would manage itself with ideas originated by many individuals within those firms. Some CEOs who write books—like Jack Welch of General Electric's *Jack*—are pretty good about sharing the credit. Others keep it all to themselves. Whether the credit is shared or not, however, no company has ever been made successful by a single visionary individual—regardless of what those individuals' books may imply.

Practicing executives and consultants suffer the same limitation in their roles as idea creators: They have other jobs. This limitation is even more constraining for practicing executives. In fact, these executive authors typically don't publish their work until the twilight of their managerial careers. For most executives, being a CEO or senior executive is simply too time-consuming to allow their acting as a guru on the side. There are some exceptions, including Richard Branson of Virgin Group. But it's usually safe to assume that the more currently active a CEO author is in managing his or her company, the greater the role of the ghostwriter in getting the book out.

Practicing managers, however, have one great virtue as idea creators: Their ideas have been successfully applied in a real organization. Managers searching for better ways to do business can be assured that the approaches advocated by practicing managers have worked at least once. Of course, the ideas could work in one context, but not another.

Practicing managers have another advantage in the challenge of distributing and publicizing ideas. They often control substantial resources that can help in the process. A corporate communications department, big publicity budgets, and many loyal minions can work wonders in launching a book. David D'Alessandro, for example, the CEO of John Hancock Insurance, had a $500,000 advertising and publicity campaign for his book *Brand Warfare*. Sumner Redstone, the CEO of Viacom, had a few advantages in publishing his book *A Passion to Win*. Simon & Schuster, part of the Viacom empire, published the book, and copies were for sale in every Blockbuster Video outlet—another Viacom business unit. Similarly, Jack Welch didn't seem to have much difficulty getting on NBC's (a unit of General Electric) *Today* show to talk about his book *Jack* or having on-camera interviews at NBC affiliate stations.

Because of these publicity advantages, it's important to separate CEO books that truly feature good business ideas from those that only tell a heroic executive's inspiring life story. Our nominee for the most idea-oriented CEO is Andrew Grove, now chairman of Intel and tied for fifty-fourth on our list. Grove's books are not puff pieces; they're full of stimulating and practical management ideas. *High Output Management,* for example, describes the application of Intel's successful manufacturing approaches to the management of people. *Only the Paranoid Survive* describes Grove's concept of the strategic inflection point, a time in a company's history when profitable markets exhaust themselves and the company must adopt radical change in products and strategies. Grove also teaches a course at Stanford Business School (Strategy and Action in the Information Processing Industry) and for many years wrote a syndicated newspaper column on management. If all CEOs were like Grove, there would be little need for business school professors, journalists, or consultants to create new business ideas.

Journalists as Gurus

Because business journalists come into considerable contact with managers and businesses, they can sometimes identify important new business ideas at an early stage. The perceptive journalist can see the makings of a new approach to business across multiple organizations, and then shape it in writings and presentations. Journalists are typically good researchers and good writers, and the magazines and newspapers for which they work provide a built-in distribution channel for their ideas.

However, the journalistic role isn't an ideal one for business idea creation. There are some fairly obvious role conflicts. First, the business reporter is primarily supposed to report on existing business practices, not develop new ideas. It's the rare journalist

who has the freedom to go beyond the existing business to identify or explore something different. For journalists, some business
must already be executing an idea before the press can report on
it. The journalistic format can also be shallow. Readers of the business press may not want to read about an idea in great detail.

Because of the orientation to reportage, business journalists
sometimes collaborate with executives in the description and distribution of ideas. *Business Week*'s John Byrne and *Fortune*'s Stratford Sherman, for example, have collaborated with GE's Jack
Welch to get out the message about the management approaches
that have made GE so successful in the 1980s and 1990s. It's safe
to assume that all the good ideas in their books didn't come from
Welch. Byrne also wrote a fascinating study of Robert McNamara
and the "scientific managers" at Ford and elsewhere. Byrne's
book *The Whiz Kids* is ostensibly a piece of business history, but
it's also a powerful warning about taking numbers too far as a
way to manage businesses. The prolific Byrne has also written
about "Chainsaw Al" Dunlap, silicone breast implants, headhunters, and leading business schools.

Tom Stewart, formerly a writer for *Fortune* and *Business 2.0*
and now the editor of the *Harvard Business Review*—and fifty-third
on our guru list—is one of the best examples of the business journalist as idea creator. He was clearly an early shaper of the
knowledge management and intellectual capital movements and
contributed to others (including reengineering) as well. Stewart
calls himself a business sociologist. A bit of a boundary spanner,
he headed a publishing company before moving to *Fortune*. In the
course of his journalistic work, he visits many companies and
discovers new ideas in the course of his meetings with them. As
he notes about knowledge management, "One of my jobs is to
find interesting stuff going on in corporations and write about it.
It was in the course of doing this—a story that I discuss in the
preface of my first book—that I stumbled across the idea of
knowledge assets. I thought it was interesting, a thread worth

pulling. . . . I picked it up from a guy who makes sausages. He said, 'Intellectual capital is usually more important than financial capital or material capital.'"

Stewart has all or most of the attributes of gurus. He gets out into the world, he writes and speaks a lot (we've encountered him at conferences from San Diego to Caracas to Abu Dhabi), he's done more than one thing. And like most gurus, he feels a role conflict at times. "The critical area in which the journalistic-thinker distinction arises when questions about what is 'on the record' and 'off the record' are not always clear. When I'm wearing my journalist hat, I hate people to be off the record. When I'm wearing my thinker hat, people aren't going to share half-baked ideas with me and think that they're going to be put in the display case in the bakery tomorrow. To a certain extent, I have had to be a little more relaxed about saying, 'I won't print this,' than I would otherwise want to be. It's simply because I am both participant and observer—but then everybody [in this guru category] is."

Just to round out the picture, Stewart's primary contribution to knowledge management was a seminal *Fortune* cover story in 1991. As Stewart noted in a column ten years later: "My story, 'Brainpower,' was, I'm 99% sure, the first time the business press wrote about intellectual capital. It's hard to recall the blank looks that greeted the phrase a decade ago, the puzzled 'You mean like patents?' queries, or the flippant 'Smart's nice, but I like money's superciliousness."[17]

Stewart later wrote *Intellectual Capital,* one of the earliest books on the topic (unfortunately, it was one of three books with that title in 1997). His journalistic roots are on display in that book; he has literally hundreds of quotes from company sources and other gurus. Stewart wrote a column for *Fortune* between 1995 and 2001, which featured many examples and facets of intellectual capital and knowledge management. Most recently, his primary focus in knowledge management has been on measurement issues.

Which Backgrounds Are the Most Common?

One interesting take on guru backgrounds is which of the four alternative professions is most likely to yield thought leaders in business. We classified each member of the top one hundred guru list by what we concluded was the primary occupation of the guru. The list contains fifty academics, thirty-six consultants, ten practicing managers, and four journalists. Academics probably have the most time to do guru work, and they are likely to rank highly on a list that includes scholarly citations. The role conflicts that journalists experience when acting as gurus probably accounts for the presence of only four journalists in the list (Malcolm Gladwell, Kevin Kelly, Tom Stewart, and George Gilder).

This issue of which professional backgrounds produce the most gurus was also addressed by Columbia University researchers Eric Abrahamson and Gregory Fairchild. They concluded that for one particular management topic—quality circles—the most prolific writers on the topic (which they define as gurus) were consultants, academics, and "technicians," which we define as practicing managers. Interestingly, more than half of the people they identified as gurus had Ph.D.'s—suggesting that many planned to become academics—but almost 40 percent came to view themselves as consultants. They also found that in the domain of quality circles, practicing managers were the first to identify the issue and publish on it, followed by the consulting, journalistic, and academic gurus.

Another, broader way of measuring the question of which guru backgrounds are most common is to analyze the backgrounds of contributors to the *Harvard Business Review (HBR)* and *MIT Sloan Management Review (SMR)*—probably the most commonly consulted sources of new business ideas, at least in the United States. We analyzed the authors of articles in 1998 and 1999, classifying them as academics, consultants, practicing managers, and journalists. The clear winners in both publications in terms of authorship frequency were academics (table 4-1). Business school

TABLE 4 - 1

Author Types in *Harvard Business Review* and *Sloan Management Review* Articles, 1998–1999

	Academics	Consultants	Managers	Journalists
HBR, 1998	64	32	31	4
HBR, 1999	70	46	44	6
SMR, 1998	35	9	6	0
SMR, 1999	48	7	2	0

academics (with a few exceptions from other parts of universities) totally dominate the pages of *SMR* and publish almost double the number of articles published by any other guru type in *HBR*. They are also the most likely group to publish full-length articles in *HBR* (as opposed to case study commentaries, interviews, or short descriptions of research). Consultants and managers are about equal in *HBR*, though consultants do better in *SMR*. Journalists (other than these journals' editors, who sometimes appear as commentators and case study authors in *HBR*) are seldom seen in either of these publications. They are more likely to be found in the business magazines for which they write and in books.

One of the most interesting issues raised by this analysis is how to classify the many hybrids who publish in these journals. Is Gary Hamel, for example, a consultant (as chairman of the consulting boutique Strategos) or an academic (as a former professor and frequent visitor at London Business School)? What of Andrew Campbell, the U.K.-based director of the Ashridge Strategic Management Centre? Since his unit is a research arm of Ashridge Management College, he has academic credentials. But he was formerly a full-time consultant at a large consulting firm and still consults widely as an individual. As the head of a small business, he might even be considered a practicing manager! The overlapping of categories was reasonably easy to handle in our analysis; we either decided on a primary category for an author or, when we occasionally could not do this, counted someone as belonging to more than one category. But more important, the hybrid nature of these individuals points out the boundary-spanning nature of gurus and perhaps also the need for new types of institutions that would comfortably house business thinkers.

It is important for idea practitioners to understand the source of new business ideas and to cultivate relationships with a select few gurus. However, idea practitioners must also keep "gurudom" in perspective. Gurus already receive a lot of attention in the business world. For the remainder of this book, we'll continue to focus primarily on idea practitioners, whom we believe are just as important, if not more so, to the successful use of business ideas. Accordingly, in chapters 5 and 6, we will look at two important forces that help filter and shape the most promising ideas: the marketplace for business ideas and the organizations themselves. By fitting the best ideas in the marketplace to his or her own organization, the idea practitioner is the dynamic and vital link between the two.

5

MARKET SAVVY

HOW IDEAS INTERACT WITH MARKETS

AS AUTHORS and book lovers, we enjoy browsing in the ever-diminishing number of used bookstores. Traveling around the world as we do, we often hunt for these shops in search of that elusive volume we have always wanted. However, the pleasures of book-finding serendipity are often mixed with pain (or are deeply disquieting) when we see the stacks of used management texts—especially when we spot one of our own! We are talking about popular and semipopular management books— the kind of volumes usually found, for example, in the *Business Week* or *New York Times* business best-seller lists. We do not mean the more scholarly books, written almost exclusively for academics and having very little direct influence on management. Unlike scholarly books, these popular books we encounter were once found on many executives' desks or in their briefcases. They were widely reviewed in the business press, discussed in meetings and conferences, and propounded by consultants. These books commanded much attention, short-lived but intense, and then quickly faded like exploded fireworks.

For those who like to buy used books online, there is further evidence of the rapid decline in business books' value. On eBay's Half.com site, for example, the following business books go for very low prices:

One Minute Manager (1981)	$1.25
The Wisdom of Teams (1992)	$1.50
Reengineering the Corporation (1994, paper)	$0.75
The Discipline of Market Leaders (1995, paper)	$0.75

Yet nonbusiness books of the same vintage usually sell for more. Paul Samuelson and William Nordhaus's *Microeconomics* textbook in paper goes for $6.90. Zick Rubin's *Psychology,* $5.25. The *AS/400 Communications Desk Reference, 1994 Edition* goes for a princely $32.00. Even the *1995 Guide to Car Shows, "Cruzin" and Auctions* brings $4.50.

What accounts for this rapid fall in popular business book prices? If these ideas were once worthy of consideration, how could they be so nearly worthless today? Were the ideas always of such low value? If so, how did they command such attention? And if they actually had value, where did the value go? Was it so temporal and contextual that it only worked for a few months in, say, 1995? Since virtually no one ever reads or purchases these old volumes, can their value be totally temporal? One comforting thought is that perhaps management knowledge is cumulative. If so, then current books would reflect and include past management knowledge. But if this is so, why do older books in other fields, where knowledge is also cumulative, retain more of their value? As the Half.com prices suggest, classic texts and even standard or everyday volumes in, say, psychology, economics, criticism, or history still sell online and in used bookshops, often at a considerable premium. What is going on here?

We would like to explain this phenomenon by discussing it within the framework of a market. Markets are universal phenomena, widely praised by ideologues as always "knowing best."

A significant portion of management knowledge, however, is strongly influenced by a particular market dynamic at work. Let us look at how this works by examining the proposed market for management ideas through a lens of market components.

Idea Buyers

Banal though it may sound, it's worth noting that the buyers of management ideas are managers. Why is this so? Shouldn't managers just do their jobs—doing what their job descriptions say, proceeding by a combination of common sense, logic, and their own individual experiences? Yet this is clearly not the case. From the 1980s onward, even the most obtuse or self-centered manager in an obscure industry would have had to deal with, at the least, quality issues, reengineering, and perhaps knowledge management. Of course, many managers—particularly the idea practitioners we focus on in this book—will have confronted even more of these movements, even if the managers themselves had not initiated these movements in their firms.

The Pressure of Uncertainty

One powerful but often unstated force lies behind most of this activity: uncertainty. We simply do not know—in the same way we know about chemical processes, for example—how to make organizations more effective, more efficient, or more innovative. This uncertainty is strongly coupled with managers' oft-noted mandate to ceaselessly and ruthlessly improve their organization's performance in some way. How do you improve the performance of an organization when there are no (or very few) scientific or verifiable rules and methods that will guarantee some success? Not unlike the personal psychotherapy markets, this gap between needs and verifiable methods and tools opens up a giant cognitive hole that many types of idea sellers try to fill.

For example, how does a manager effect change in an organization? Is there just one or even just a few proven ways of doing this? If this were so, organizations needing or seeking change would seek out a proven method and simply implement it. If not approach A, then maybe B or E or even R would work, and firms needing change would thereby change in the desired direction. However, even a whole alphabet of approaches would not come close to encompassing how many methods or approaches exist in this one specific marketplace. By a quick survey, we have found at least 680 books and literally thousands of articles on this subject. Virtually every major (and most smaller) consulting firm also offers a set of ideas, tools, and methods for managing change in their clients. Clearly, whatever empirically verifiable knowledge that exists in this field is either deeply fragmented and held in narrow, obscure, and highly academic publications or does not exist at all. Success at organizational change is just too idiosyncratic and contextual. When a change management program is initiated in an organization, a manager will have no single or "true" verifiable accepted methods to work with. He or she will face a bewildering gamut of approaches, which vary wildly in cost, complexity, methodology, and time expenditures. However, two things still remain true: The manager will have to act and will somehow have to choose an approach to take.

The Pressure of Coercion

Grounded in this persistent sense of uncertainty are several powerful forces continuously at work, strongly influencing managers to search and "purchase" ideas. One of these is what Paul DiMaggio and Walter Powell call coercive processes.[1] These are the pressures that managers feel from others who have the power and clout to influence their choice of what ideas can be used for improvement. A moment's reflection will allow any manager to see who constitutes this group—capital markets analysts, members of the organization's board of directors, important vendors and customers, and even journalists. Similar to the message of the other processes we will mention, the "message" these people convey is usually couched in an appeal to efficiency: "We've heard that (choose your movement) is helping firms improve their performance—how come you're not doing it?" When such a message comes from a person with either economic or bureaucratic power, a manager needs to devise a fairly strong and convincing rebuttal for not undertaking at least a study of the proposed movement.

One of the idea practitioners we interviewed, Chris Hoenig, has worked on both sides of the coercion table. As head of information technology for the General Accounting Office, Hoenig spent five years attempting to define best IT practices and persuading U.S. government agencies to adopt them. By the time he left the job, the federal government had adopted major legislation on IT, CIO roles in agencies, a Y2K remediation effort, diagnostic and quality programs, and many other initiatives and changes. Hoenig describes the way these ideas spread: "The brushfire was really fed by legislation. We found a congressman who was willing to sponsor it. We drafted the legislation. We got everyone involved around the government—built a network. Once the legislation was drafted, we worked on implementing it and developed diagnostic tools that any of the agencies could use. . . . We had cover so that it eventually evolved from a very small idea to something that tens of thousands of people were using and building on to do business differently." By mobilizing those coercive pressures, Hoenig very successfully brought about change.

Consulting organizations, which have long been aware of the link between landing a bylined article in *Harvard Business Review* and sales revenues, understand this connection between legitimization and value. But these forces act on managers as well, such as when a set of ideas become legitimized by selective institutions such as journals, business schools, think tanks, consulting firms, professional organizations, or individual gurus. These groups often unleash what Lynne Zucker calls the contagion of legitimacy.[2] In other words, attention from various business institutions lends credence to an idea, which engenders more attention and hence even more credence, or legitimization. This "contagion of legitimacy" emboldens businesspeople to carry forth these ideas right to a manager's desk for "immediate action."

The Pressure of Legitimization

The power of legitimization is very important in leading a manager to buy into an idea. Its appeal is often the much mentioned "voice of authority" that sellers strive mightily to obtain. Such cognitive authority often has a power approaching religion or social custom in convincing managers to act in a specific way. Aliana Rozenek, an idea practitioner who has worked in industries as dissimilar as aluminum can manufacturing and financial service, makes this observation: "If you look at all these ideas— from quality to reengineering and so on—they all have a common thread. They use human creativity, human spirit, human potential in an inclusive way to make people and products better."

But how does a supposedly imaginative and individualistic phenomenon like an idea become inclusive and socialized in the way she describes? It is perceived as authoritative. The difference between a voice of authority and a "plain ol' voice" is that the authoritative voice is amplified through an attention-getting bullhorn, one that conveys legitimacy. The bullhorns that caught Rozenek's ear were books—"particularly those written by Deming"—case studies, and research output from respected think tanks like The Tavistock Institute and the American Society for Quality Improvement.

The Pressure of Conformity

After coercion and legitimization, there are also adaptive (or what our theorist friends sometimes call "mimetic") pressures. These, too, are well-documented and powerful pressures on managers to conform to what others in their industry are doing, or alternatively, to what a "legitimized," successful firm is doing. We all know how selected firms become (with considerable help from the firms themselves!) paragons of performance—looked up to by others both within and outside their specific industry. General Electric is a good current example. In six out of the eight firms one of us met with in 2002, the managers brought up GE in some regard—but always holding it up as a model to be imitated. In the 1990s, IBM, Toyota, Citicorp, and even General Motors occupied this role.

Touted, if not invented, by gurus as models of management, these companies play a very useful role. They embody, in an exemplary form, the often-abstract concepts being sold by the idea industry. There is a great deal of difference between listening to an abstract discussion on the learning organization and hearing how GE embeds and uses learning at its executive teaching facility in Crotonville, New York. As Voltaire might say if he were alive today, these firms would have to be invented if they didn't already exist.

This process of identifying exemplars has given rise to a semiformal kind of advice known as benchmarking. In benchmarking, an individual tells stories, often complete with numbers, of other firms that have achieved some performance standards that his or her own firm should strive to emulate. Firms often take to this advice (like so much other advice) in different ways—from strict imitation to proximate imitation to using the stories for inspiration rather than strict adoption. For example, Ford spent billions of dollars trying to strictly achieve Toyota's warranty recall rate. Though Ford never achieved this, it did considerably improve some of its own quality processes in its attempt. Quite a few firms have tried to become as quality driven as Motorola (another onetime exemplar firm) was seen to be. Having won the coveted Baldrige Award for performance excellence and therefore gaining a powerful sign of legitimization, Motorola was besieged by firms and consultants anxious to learn its quality ideas. The company actually had to open an office just to focus on "visiting firemen," as did almost every other Baldrige winner.

Interestingly, although academics speak often of other companies having adopted ideas as a legitimizing force, several idea practitioners in our interviews did not consider it a strong factor.

Dave Barrow at BP was one such person: "I can't feel assured that just because another company is implementing a new business approach that it's going to be pertinent to our context. For example, a lot of companies are implementing customer relationship management software. There is much hype, and I think that it might have some merit for BP someday, but simply hearing that other companies are pursuing it isn't really compelling to me—it doesn't compel me to look at it for our business right now."

Alex Bennett, chief knowledge officer of the U.S. Navy in 2000, when we interviewed her, argues that an idea's being popular within other organizations doesn't matter to the navy, but having clear examples of success elsewhere does make an important difference: "I find it extremely valuable to have successes occurring in other organizations (both inside and out of government) and use these examples fully and completely. There is high value in external validation of internal implementation ideas."

The Pressure of Economic Heuristics

Social scientists often emphasize a factor called organizational bounded rationality. Bounded rationality was first used by economist and Nobel Prize winner Herbert Simon to help describe why traditional economic models of human activity were flawed. These models had a built-in assumption that people looked at all the available information before making an economic decision. Simon and his cohorts pointed out just how impossible this is, both practically and cognitively. In the absence of doing a thorough and time-consuming search, we all develop and use various shortcuts, home-grown rules of thumb (often called heuristics) to allow us to make more efficient decisions. These mental shortcuts place a boundary on a broader, completely rational viewpoint for making decisions, thus the term *bounded rationality*. For example, we often use brand-name products for just this reason. Who has the time, means, or energy to seek out the best detergent?

Now think about how this process works for executives at, say, an eighty-thousand-employee, globally dispersed maker of home appliances. Let us imagine they feel the need, because of higher-than-usual production costs relative to competitors and a concurrent lack of innovative processes, to institute a change management program. The CEO says that she wants to use the best proven methods to do this. What does this mean? Can her executives visit all the industry's major firms that have had some success in change management, or even firms outside the industry, to investigate what they did? Under the pressure to "get something done" efficiently, the executives are likely to turn to a consulting firm that has experience at managing this type of change, having used it at many large companies. Perhaps an article or book on the topic will be supplied. A rational method is then employed, diagnostic tools are applied, and recommendations are advanced. By choosing a reputable firm, managers can claim to have complied with the CEO's request, and in doing so they are spared an onerous and perhaps impossible task.

Several idea practitioners we interviewed reported that they sometimes take advantage of the reputations of gurus or external consultants in order to bring credibility to ideas they'd like to make happen. As one noted, "I look for what the academic leaders are doing and saying, and I try to understand that point of view and introduce it to the right senior leaders. For example, John Doe [here he named a particular guru] is somebody who has quite a lot of credibility with my company's senior leadership, and I want to continue to have a good relationship with John so that he can help me get my job done by supporting our approach. I'm sitting inside a closed system here, and it's important to have somebody on the outside recognizing what I'm doing."

The Pressure of Bandwagons

The last point to make about pressures that move buyers is the good reputation granted those who implement apparently progressive ideas. We've already described the research by Barry Staw and Lisa Epstein of the University of California at Berkeley in this regard. They studied a large cohort of firms that had bought into ideas on quality, empowerment, and teams and had attempted to put the ideas into action. Shaw and Epstein found that "companies associated with these popular management techniques did not have higher economic performance. Nevertheless these same companies were more admired, perceived to be more innovative and rated higher in management quality."[3]

The pressure to jump on the business idea bandwagon, as described in the preceding statement by Shaw and Epstein, is embedded in management practice. It is well known that even the perception that a firm is undertaking a well-thought-of program can produce beneficial effects on recruitment, stock performance, and customer acquisition and retention. Much of corporate PR efforts are aimed at getting this message out for just these reasons.

Of course this is not at all to say that such programs are not worthy. They often are. But what economists call externalities—often unplanned or unanticipated effects that come about from a more direct action—are often not too far from idea buyers' minds.

Idea Sellers

There is a large, very powerful, largely unregulated and unreported, fragmented yet global industry that affects all our lives. Lest you think we have succumbed to conspiracy theory, we'll quickly explain that we are talking about the advice industry.[4] Largely a part of the professional services industry, the advice industry generally comprises consulting firms, investment banks, business schools, law firms, rating agencies, newsletter publishers, solo consulting practitioners, marketing and design services, many technology vendors, and IT service providers. What these various organizations do is develop, codify, promote, market, and sell advice to management. The development and maturation of this industry has had an enormous effect on the size and importance of business idea markets.

The size of this industry is unknown, although estimates can range anywhere from 8 to 27 percent of the U.S. gross domestic product.[5] The industry includes some obvious, large players (e.g., McKinsey & Company, Accenture, Shearman & Sterling, Jones Day, IBM Global Services, Gartner Group, Goldman Sachs, Harvard Business School, and Morgan Stanley). A few smaller and independent-minded players, however, have an influence sometimes equal to that of a whole firm. For example, Peter Drucker arguably has had more impact on business and management, with more people and firms, than have all the employees of any large advice firm combined.

What all these disparate players have in common is that they are playing in a dynamic market in which new ideas embedded in products and services need to be developed, as the market demands it and as the internal economies of the sellers also demand it. This is more than just supply meeting demand. It is a good example of supply also creating demand. Management uncertainty creates demand, but so do the varying strategies of sellers to create demand where it may be latent or dormant or even nonexistent. Organizations have undoubtedly heard about reengineering or knowledge management, for example, and then adopted the ideas without previously knowing that they needed them.

Obviously not all the advice sold involves management ideas, though more of it does than one would initially think. Often, even seemingly arcane ideas concerning, say, an IT application, a point of law, or a market research study use the rhetoric of management ideas. For example, law firms in the late 1990s pushed their expertise in mergers, acquisitions, and public offerings, often wrapped in the rhetoric of the "new economy." In the software industry, companies sell database applications as customer relationship management systems to exploit the increasing interest in winning and retaining customers through having more or better knowledge about them. In the software industry, thought leadership is a well-understood term, and companies strive to promote their software as a vehicle for addressing a business idea. One of the idea practitioners we interviewed, who works in marketing for an e-commerce software firm, described the issue: "We started out as an e-commerce software firm, but then everybody was in that category, so we had to evolve our *thought leadership*. We became a 'content management' firm, and helped to define that space. But then it evolved into the 'portals' space, which got very crowded. So now we are trying to focus on 'customer self-serv-ice,' but I'm afraid that we're not doing enough to define the ap-proach and persuade customers to adopt it."

We could go on and on with examples, but our point is that management ideas are usually imperialistic in intent and in effect. They spread both to many sectors of the economy and to govern-ment agencies as well. As detailed in chapters 7 and 8, for exam-ple, both reengineering and knowledge management had, and are having, extended lives in global corporations, nongovernmental organizations, and government agencies throughout the world.

But what is actually being sold—and in what form? We would parse the way advice is offered, beyond just the simple symbolic ideas that become key words, as falling into two distinct cate-gories: analytics and narratives.

Analytics

In some ways the first mainstay of the business idea industry, analytics, is the simplest to explain. There has always been a sub-stantial element of technical expertise offered to management from its earliest incarnations in the late nineteenth century (or even earlier—some say that Jean Rodolphe Perronet, a Parisian civil engineer, first gave this kind of advice to a manufacturer of pins in 1760). This expertise grew out of the engineering disci-pline, with perhaps some ingredients taken from accounting and applied economics. In fact, much of this early work was done under the name of industrial economics. It usually was statistical in form—analyzing, through sophisticated statistical practices, sit-uations that were complex and amenable to improvements in this fashion. Frederick Taylor and Frank Gilbreth, two of the earliest management consultants, applied statistical tools to work pro-cesses at the end of the nineteenth century and the beginning of the twentieth. Arthur D. Little and Roger Griffin, chemists at about the same time, formed the first consulting firm to apply engineering and scientific research findings to business applications.

As time went on, these analytical techniques multiplied, as consultants used more and more sophisticated mathematics to focus on complex subjects such as control, production, logistics, and even marketing. With World War II came the development of operations research. And with the coming of commercially available computer power in the mid-1950s, we began to see how these technical tools could be used to produce very sophisticated models of complex operations. PCs and off-the-shelf software now allow every M.B.A. (or even just technically inclined managers) to do most of these analyses, as well as many other operations undreamed of in earlier decades.

The commodification of these analytic techniques has inevitably reduced the premium that firms are willing to pay for them. This creates pressures for the advice industry to create new, ever-more-complex systems and ideas to present to clients that they themselves would find difficult to do. The commodification also creates an incentive for advice sellers to package their ideas within the context of their own experiences with other clients, which is more difficult to commodity.

Narratives

The most important way in which ideas and experiences are communicated from sellers to buyers is through narratives—the second mainstay of the idea industry. In the 1990s and onward, much has been written on the way that stories convey information and messages from person to person and from institutions to people.[6] Narratives provide a rule structure within a recognizable, action-oriented context. Idea sellers will almost always tell a story that imbeds a rule—when a firm did this (e.g., reengineering, quality management, knowledge management), they got this result (improved performance). Details, personalities, humor, politics, leadership, "blood, sweat, and tears" are all added to the fundamental rule, but the heart of these idea-selling narratives always boils down to some performance-enhancing action (or why tell them?).

Narratives are seen as somewhat more credible coming from an older and more senior practitioner. Of course, there is nothing much new in this observation. African griots are mostly older tribesmen who tell tribal histories as stories and lessons, as are the Balkan "singers of tales."[7] People in general give greater credence to more senior storytellers, perhaps because older tellers have lived through more events and have refined their stories to their essentials, or because they have gained the wisdom to emphasize what stories to tell, to whom, and to what effect. In selling ideas, people use stories to emphasize the more tacit aspects of implementing an idea-based program. After all, if the work was entirely explicit and easily documented and understood, then a firm wouldn't need outsiders to provide advice. Stories often help convey this tacit side of rules and also the practitioner's possession of these tacit skills.

Another way stories are used is to show the network power of the seller. Sellers will explain that they learned a technique from a famous professor or consultant or some heroic managers. Or perhaps the story is based on the presumed aggregated stories of all the sellers' colleagues. Large advice-industry organizations often proclaim in their advertisements and in client proposals that their approach is based on aggregate firm experiences. Advertisements proclaim something like, "Hire us, and you get the experience and know-how of fifty thousand brilliant employees." And the stories told gain in power from having come from such diverse experiences.

Idea Market Channels

We would be remiss if we didn't mention the sector of the advice industry, huge in itself, that often allows specific ideas to reach their intended customers. After all, a thinker can sit in his or her office and have great thoughts of bringing hyperefficient practices to some of the more sluggish organizations. But how will the supplier and intended buyer ever meet? And though we've already mentioned how firms monitor each other's activities, very specific idea offerings are often found through public idea markets.

The most important institutions at work here—publishing, conferences, and education—play a key role in making the idea market. In addition to the role played by idea buyers and sellers, another role, that of the idea broker, can take various forms. As we'll discuss, brokers facilitate the smooth functioning of markets and channels.

Publishing   There is something magical and elusive, but undeniably powerful, in print material. Reading about ideas in a journal or book gives the ideas a weightedness, a gravitas, that just doesn't exist when they are heard in a conversation or read on a screen. As we have been stressing here, ideas are evaluated and understood within their social context. In the business ideas market, it matters that sellers are actually published and it matters where they publish.

Publications have a clear role in legitimizing ideas and in publicizing and providing credentials for the idea seller. As discussed in chapter 8, a cover story in *Fortune* on intellectual capital and knowledge gave a strong impetus to the whole knowledge management movement. The *Wall Street Journal, Business Week,* and *Fortune* all published several key stories on process reengineering, and *The Economist* followed suit in both subjects. Reengineering, the balanced scorecard, activity-based costing, real options analysis, attention management, level-five leadership, and many other new business ideas have been published at an early stage in their lives in the *Harvard Business Review.*

The number of journals, magazines, and book publishers that can help launch a movement is limited by necessity. The business magazines, such as *Fortune, Business Week, Forbes,* and *The Economist* have certainly played a role in credentialing individuals and firms, as well as temporarily focusing attention on ideas. The more substantial and academic, but still readable, business journals—*Harvard Business Review, MIT Sloan Management Review,* and *California Management Review*—are much more effective in legitimizing ideas in the first place. The articles in these journals are either peer-reviewed or intensely examined by experienced editors. These journals are also quite competitive, rejecting four or five articles for every one accepted. These criteria also apply to the much more scholarly management journals such as *Administrative Science Quarterly, Management Science, Organization Science,* and the various publications of the Academy of Management. Articles in these journals are occasionally read by businesspeople and even cited in popular management texts (such as this one, we hope). Nevertheless, they are written by, and for, academics and make few concessions on accessibility and readability for the manager. We have never met an executive or a manager who regularly reads these scholarly articles.

Books also provide a means of selling ideas. Not too long ago, management books were meant to be timeless. Peter Drucker's books were written with this aim and have proven to be at least very long-lived; almost all of them are still in print. But now, about two thousand business books are published each year. Lately, more books are often rushed into print to catch a particular management wave. Once the reengineering movement was under way, twenty-six books were published on the movement within a couple of years. Although many of these were slapped together and had little or nothing to add (neither analytics nor stories) to the subject, the motivation for the authors was clear—legitimization through the publication of the book.

However, there are status distinctions between publishers, too. Acting as effective legitimizing agents, certain publishing houses and the presses of major business schools are expanding their book lists to tap this idea market. The university presses at Harvard, MIT, Stanford, and Oxford have particularly high volume. Even very mainstream publishers such as Doubleday, Harper-

Collins, Basic, Wiley, McGraw-Hill, and Random House have an avid interest in this very elastic business-idea market.

Education   In the 1980s and 1990s, executive education became a very substantial business in itself and has proven to be the financial salvation for many business schools. Schools usually can charge anything from $2,000 to $25,000 for a short-term, intense course on a focused topic or idea. Perhaps a mix of forty or fifty middle managers, senior managers, or both assemble at the school. They are suitably wined, dined, and instructed by presumed experts in the subject area and are sent on their way with a certificate attesting to their attendance and learning. This latter benefit almost always finds its way to the attendee's résumé, adding a more personal incentive to the standard justifications for attendance. Business schools also provide more customized executive education courses, hand-crafted to the specific needs of an organization. These types of services are usually more broad-based (e.g., Finance and Accounting for the Nonfinancial Executive) or idiosyncratic to the company, and subsequently play less of a role in our story.

Idea-based programs (in which, in the spirit of full disclosure, we occasionally participate as instructors) also perform three powerful functions in the idea markets. They provide further credentialing of individual experts; they develop cases that add legitimization and texture to the subject; and they educate cadres of practitioners—many of whom go forth and spread the good words for the cause.

We use the term "further" credentialing because usually a professional will establish himself or herself as an expert by publishing a book or key article before actually developing and offering a course. A good example is Clay Christensen of the Harvard Business School. His justifiably very well-received book, *The Innovator's Dilemma,* created a groundswell of interest in innovation and how an organization can become more innovative or better take advantage of innovations they already have. Within a year of the book's achieving its success, the Harvard Business School was offering executive education courses featuring Clay himself, as well as some colleagues and associates. Although the process has a touch of magic to it (as do many of the things we are talking about here), the very act of spending time with the idea generator (even if he or she hasn't developed much new material) seems to give an added boost to the guru's value in the eyes of the attendee. Part of this can be explained by the practitioner coming back to his office and saying something like "I just took a three-day course on building the innovative organization. Boy, the teacher was terrific—she had examples, cases, methods, techniques, and so forth—and you could feel the excitement in the air. I also learned a huge amount from the other students—what they're doing or not doing in their organizations."

In any case, it's usually a good bet that the guru will be asked to speak or consult with some of the attending firms, further adding to the person's résumé and increasing his or her legitimization ("I've consulted to A, B, and C firms"). Economists sometimes speak of "increasing returns to reputation"—those who are well known become more well known by having been well known in the first place—and executive education provides a good channel for this to occur.

Cases or narratives are essential to an idea's becoming a movement. They encapsulate, elaborate, and provide the impetus for action. "Did you hear [or read] about what BP did with knowledge management?" was a critical question asked by idea sellers in the growth of the knowledge management movement, mainly because they could use several potent stories and cases to respond to this query. Since writing substantial cases is a time-consuming process, it usually is done by academics at universities or academics temporarily housed in consulting organizations. In addition, because academics are often perceived as being noncompetitive (at least within an industry context), it's therefore safe to discuss company affairs with them. Another incentive for the firm is that case-based narratives travel quite far. Since cases in general tend to be adulatory or neutral at worst (managers must

sign off on them before they are distributed), the good news about
an organization's work is spread around the world by consultants,
professors in executive education courses, and researchers in general. These cases often get abridged into stories that are picked
up by the more sophisticated business journalists, and can then
reach many more people.

We know of no good estimate of how many managers take
courses that are more focused on an idea or movement, in contrast to a more generic course on, say, accounting or marketing.
After discussing this with several program directors, however, we
estimate that between three and five thousand annually take
idea-based courses. Since usually one person (or at most two or
three) from an organization attends, these attendees can quickly
create a wave of charged-up practitioners ready to move their organizations forward. Of course, not everyone "gets religion." But
the enthusiasm of a credentialed guru and the prestige and authority of an educational institution are hard to resist. In addition, commitment to taking such a course—getting approval to
spend the tuition, time off, etc.—would often by itself bring some
zeal and purposeful action in its wake. Who wants to be known
as someone who spent the time and expense and returned to
work with a shrug, or a bland "It was OK"?

These students, then, almost all senior middle to senior management, play a significant role in helping to further legitimize
a movement after it has gotten started. They help to make the
idea real by virtue of their status and power within an organization, their passion for the subject (however short-term it may be),
their ability to institutionalize the movement (by creating budgets, goals, departments, or functions), and the contagion factor
they generate through their zeal. Their passion is often caught by
others, thus further spreading the movement.

Conferences   No account of the idea market infrastructure
would be complete without a word about the seemingly ubiquitous conferences for which we all get notices. (Yes, we speak
at these, too.) These events help more in the initial stages of

building an idea movement. They create an initial buzz among managers, since conferences are so thoroughly marketed (mass mailings of one or even two million are not unknown). Conferences also help credential gurus—who are usually consultants or senior executives, or occasionally academics or journalists—by focusing on them as keynote speakers. In particular, conferences also focus on "leading practitioners" of a movement, that is, those first participants who help define the movement via speaking at these conferences. Many of the idea practitioners we interviewed for this book fall into this category. At some firms, such as The World Bank, Buckman Labs, BP, Johnson & Johnson, Skandia, and Xerox, practitioners who helped define the knowledge management movement gathered their renown in just this way.

These conferences also help create a critical mass of enthusiasts. Charging anywhere from $750 to about $3,000, they are usually cheaper—and a bit lower down the status ladder—than executive education courses, are not at all selective in admissions, and grant no usable certificates of attendance. They do, however, offer significant networking opportunities for attendees, since these events sometimes draw up to several thousand people for a few days of talks, meals, drinks, and the like. Many conferences have now begun to refer to a "networking lunch" or a "break for networking" in their schedules. Attendees come home with handouts and binders containing presentations of organizational stories and perhaps some analytics. At some conferences, attendees may even arrange a visit or two, to "kick the tires" of the presenting firm. Often institutionalized as benchmarking, these exercises help to legitimize among others a leading organization practice at a firm by showing it at work and in context.

On the other hand, conferences have a substantial commercial aura and flavor quite distinct from executive education programs. In contrast to the educational programs (which sometimes lag too far behind the development of idea-based movements), the best conferences crop up at the very beginning of a movement, before there is much besides a few stories to tell. Several of our idea practitioners remembered that they were at our first conference on knowledge management, which took place in 1995—and several seemed to feel that everything went downhill thereafter. The relentless marketing with its accompanying hyperbole and other hoopla sometimes can actually discredit a movement or lead it down paths of extreme consulting and vendor hype. This certainly happened with the reengineering and knowledge management movements we elaborate on later chapters. On balance, however, conferences can be seen as part medicine show and part educational experience. The results usually do more good than harm in creating momentum for an idea movement.

Idea Brokers

As in other markets, brokers play a pivotal role by matching buyers and sellers. There are many types of brokers, providing different types of services. Some brokers, such as the speaker bureaus representing the gurus who present to conferences and company meetings, actually match idea buyers and sellers. Firms like the Leigh Bureau and Leading Thoughts help a presentation client to identify, approach, and shape the presentation of a particular idea creator or guru.

Other forms of brokers provide advice on which seller of advice to choose. Like the research groups within investment banks, consulting and IT industry analyst firms such as Gartner Group, Forrester Research, and Kennedy Information evaluate the ideas of different management idea providers so that buyers can make a more educated decision. Consulting firms, in particular, try to impress these firms' analysts with their ideas, expertise, and ability to help clients implement. Gartner Group's Magic Quadrant, which ranks services and software firms both on their "completeness of vision" (i.e., the quality of their ideas) and their "ability to execute" (i.e., their ability to assist clients in implementing the ideas) is a familiar and highly valued rating system for both buyers and sellers. There is even a firm that advises on which advice firm best covers the advice industry. Outsell, a California-based firm offering perhaps the ultimate service of the information age, ranks the different industry analysts on their coverage of the IT industry.

At times, idea practitioners act as another type of broker. They may not be the actual buyer, that is, the sponsoring executive who pays the bill for the implementation of the idea. Nor do they have to be the actual user, that is, the manager who implements the idea in his or her part of the business. When the idea practitioner connects external providers of ideas with the sponsors and users within firms, however, he or she needs to act as broker to do some selling. Mohi Ahmed at Fujitsu Microelectronics, for example, believes that one of his most important functions after identifying an idea is to rapidly find both a sponsor and a user for it. Like many good brokers, he can then withdraw after the initial sale from the transaction, and move on to another idea and another set of buyers.

Which Ideas Will Fly?

How should idea practitioners evaluate the ideas they encounter in these various markets and channels? This question can be addressed in a theoretical way or in light of the idea's fit for a specific organization. Business book reviewers, for example, generally rely on three theoretical standards for evaluating business ideas: functionality, intellectual rigor, and style. (See sidebar for definitions and examples of each standard.) Together these three standards give idea practitioners a provisional model for sizing up whether an idea is any good—whether encountered in a journal, at a conference, or in a book.

For example, we'd argue that the ideas expressed in Jim Collins's *Good to Great* have a nice balance of intellectual rigor, functionality, and style—and we're happy to observe that the book has been on business best-seller lists since it came out (in

What the Critics Say

We looked at hundreds of business book reviews and found three basic criteria that reviewers use to evaluate a new management idea. Together these form the backbone of a simple evaluative model.

Functionality: The functionality standard is prescriptive, action oriented, and practical, and emphasizes measurement. Here are some typical reviews for books emphasizing functionality: "You need this book if you are measuring anything," "offers potent remedies," "emphasizes the implementation of strategy rather than its formulation," "an actionable blueprint."

Style: The style standard is descriptive, entertaining and story-oriented, aesthetic and emotional in focus. Books presenting ideas with style generate these kinds of reviews: "The arguments are delivered with humor and passion," "a wide range of case examples and a well-organized presentation bring clarity and precision to a daunting subject," "wonderful with metaphors—uses them brilliantly to capture the major tensions between global forces," and "the story clearly illustrates the grand vision."

Intellectual Rigor: This standard is applied to books based on a fresh synthesis of information or a comprehensive look at an existing body of knowledge. Ideas judged for their intellectual rigor are research oriented and are empirical or data driven. Examples of reviews of books that show intellectual rigor are these: "A powerful foundation: high-level vision . . . business case studies and deep empirical research, western and Japanese perspectives," "based on their field research and experience in companies," "data that explains why some leaders succeed and others fail," "the empirical analysis makes this an impressive book."

other words, virtue has been rewarded). In terms of intellectual rigor, the research study behind *Good to Great* involved a fifteen-year analysis of companies that outperformed their industries, combined with a matched-pair study of companies in the same industries as the outperformers who didn't adopt "good to great" ideas.

Collins's book also has a functional dimension. He and his research team clearly know their way around companies and are able to relate what's going on in laymen's terms. Each chapter has a clear summary of key points and findings. Analyses penetrate quickly to the heart of the matter. For example, he describes the late Upjohn, one of the not-so-good companies, in a nutshell: "[Upjohn fell] into a pattern of selling the future ('The future never looked brighter') and hyping the potential of new products. But results failed to match the hype. Upjohn stock became volatile and speculative—up and down, up and down again—as it sold the sizzle, but never delivered the steak. Later, like a gambler at Las Vegas, it threw its chips on 'savior products,' such as Rogaine baldness cure. Persistent product problems, with Halcion and others, exacerbated the swings. [The company eventually] succumbed to restructuring disease and merged with Pharmacia."[8]

Good to Great also has style. The book is full of interesting and personal anecdotes about great leaders such as Admiral James Stockdale, Winston Churchill, and the quiet CEOs of Collins's exemplary companies. Much of the content is phrased as an instance of Isaiah Berlin's famous dichotomy of foxes versus hedgehogs. In this book, the hedgehogs win handily—and stylishly.

A model based on theoretical standards like rigor, functionality, and style can provide a good first line of defense for those who encounter a significant volume of new business ideas each year. But from a practitioner perspective, this type of model is limited; it doesn't go far enough addressing the will-it-fit question. Accordingly, in chapter 6, we will look at the approaches that idea practitioners use to filter and fit ideas to their organization.

Joel Kurtzman, Idea Practitioner

Several idea practitioners we studied are also idea developers and creators. Among this group, few are as prolific as Joel Kurtzman, the Global Lead Partner for Thought Leadership and Innovation at PricewaterhouseCoopers (none has a lengthier title, though).

Kurtzman is responsible for both developing and bringing new ideas—from new performance measures to e-business—into his firm and striving to get them accepted. He also manages the company's Technology Center in California, which does technology forecasts and analysis.

After graduating from the University of California with a degree in history, Kurtzman started out as a researcher with several non-governmental organizations, focusing on global and regional economic issues. He then went on to work for the *New York Times* as a business editor and columnist and the *Harvard Business Review* as editor. Before taking his current position at PricewaterhouseCoopers, he worked for several consulting and research organizations.

Kurtzman has written or edited an astonishing eighteen books ranging from two novels to volumes focusing on the death of money, how markets really work, and "futurecasting." In his spare time, he reviews business books on CNN and edits a new business encyclopedia.

6

WILL IT FIT?

FIND IDEAS THAT FIT YOUR ORGANIZATION . . . THEN SELL THEM

THERE ARE MANY IDEAS in the marketplace, but only a small subset of these ideas will be a good fit for your organization at a given time. Some ideas are aimed at innovation, whereas your organization's leadership may currently be focused on effectiveness. Other ideas may seem groundbreaking, but are irrelevant to your firm's existing focus on gaining incremental operational efficiencies. Organizations need a smart, trusted, and no-nonsense person to sort through it all.

This is a sentiment we heard repeatedly as we listened to CEOs and senior executives in focus groups discuss their expectations and experiences with management ideas. While we were there in purpose to offer our analyses to the business publication that had organized the proceedings, we became energized and extra-attentive as we heard participants in each of the four groups describe the vital role a select individual (or two) plays inside their organizations. Without any prompting, but using similar conceptual language, participants would mention an employee who acts as their organization's "idea filter," "idea funnel," "idea gatekeeper," or "intelligent filter." They discussed the way this individual was able to align real and pressing organizational needs with a particular idea, and how their organization would likely benefit from developing more of this kind of talent.

While close to "idea practitioner," their verbiage wasn't exactly ours. But their choice of words precisely captured the evaluative "filtering" skills that idea practitioners bring to bear inside their organizations, skills that we call *translation, harmonization,* and *timing.* Importantly, these filtering skills form the basis for a successful sales campaign and implementation, which we describe at the end of the chapter.

Translation

Idea practitioners know whether their culture tends to be experimental, whether it is technology-driven, whether it has hard or soft performance metrics. They understand their current business climate and their organization's strategy and structure. They can tell whether an idea needs little modification or significant modification to work inside their firm. According to Lowell Bryan, a combination of idea practitioner and banking guru now working on implementing knowledge management at McKinsey, idea practitioners sometimes need to think like offensive linemen, who understand that forward motion isn't possible without good blocking.

Bryan works in what he describes as a highly analytical firm, one where employees expect ideas to be rigorously researched and add clear value. His sense of what makes a good fit is, from the start, tempered by the kind of organization he works in. At his organization, ideas must purport to solve a specific organizational problem and be fact-based and logical. If the idea doesn't open itself up to these analytical criteria, he knows it won't work: "Analytics, facts, logic—that's the direction my vision takes as I look at an idea. Does the idea address a problem specific enough for people to get it? Does the idea take on identifiable economic problems? Will there be return on investment? This is a consulting organization, so when I consider an idea, I'd better think like a consultant."

Other idea practitioners we interviewed like Josh Plaskoff and Tony DiMarco eloquently describe this as a translation process. The manager imagines how an idea gleaned from a third-party source—a presentation, a book, an article—would fit in at his or her firm. Both Plaskoff and DiMarco point out that during translation, the idea practitioner breathes life into the idea, readying that which is abstracted and intellectually static for dynamic action. Something that is primarily a book-worthy idea becomes an idea ready for action. DiMarco, who discovered and fine-tuned his understanding of the translation process while introducing new marketing ideas to IBM, now teaches it to managers and executives as a consultant. He describes his introduction of Jim Collins's concept of level-five leadership to a group of clients: "I used Collins's article as a provocative object. The idea provokes them to imagine not only how they might integrate a new idea in their organization; it motivates them to create their own idea in light of their own understanding of their organization."

DiMarco's description is supported by Bryan's, which emphasizes that a good idea must be open to appropriation by a firm: "Evaluating ideas is an interactive process. It's the interaction that makes the ideas better, more specific, more targeted. I do lots of fine-tune adjustments—in some cases major adjustments—based upon these interactions. Throughout my interaction with an idea, I am testing to see whether it is capable of becoming a 'knowledge object'—an idea that can be conveyed within my firm without the presence of the original source."

When an idea practitioner weighs an idea's translatability, he or she must ask some broad, hypothetical questions: What is the likelihood that the idea could be successfully integrated into the firm? Is the idea something that the firm could take ownership of? Would my firm even want to own the idea?

To answer these questions, the idea practitioner must have a firm grasp of the firm's business climate and idiosyncratic biases, which often determine whether an idea is translatable. Forces like whether a firm is document-centered or person-centered, risk-taking or risk-averse, can make or break an idea when placed into an organizational context.

For example, when Charles Seeley left Warner Lambert for Intel in 1999, he quickly recognized the differences between the two firms. Both are conservative organizations that adopt new business ideas slowly and scrupulously. But Intel has a strong technology bias, one that Seeley has to consider in an unexpected way when introducing a new strategic initiative: "Prior to my joining Intel, knowledge management was promoted across the organization, but at a theoretical and abstract level. Intel people love technology. So, knowledge management at Intel (and many other companies) ended up being equated with 'cool' technologies, document or content management tools. The only concrete knowledge management activities were around these. No strategic plans for knowledge management had been prepared up to that point. I advocated a pilot project to prove the value of capabilities to enable locating expertise as the basis for tacit knowledge transfer. That pilot has now been launched in several organizations."

Seeley saw that knowledge management had been adopted in his firm strictly in terms of Intel's technology biases, not around other potentially strategic or high-value areas. As he was initiating new and strategic knowledge management ideas, he understood the firm's tendency to think of new ideas as "cool, new technologies." Seeley wanted to promote an idea—tacit knowledge transfer—that went against the grain of the firm's technology bias. He therefore couched it in terms of the expertise locator tools that would help to make it possible.

One idea practitioner, who asked not to be named, was a managing director of a midsized technology consulting firm. Her firm competed in an industry that was hurt badly when the technology bubble burst in 2000. Demand was down, and competition among sellers in this newly overcrowded marketplace was intense. The firm had "a core competence that is very unique in our space." By the winter of 2002, however, the firm had just gone through several rounds of layoffs—four in the past twelve months—and morale was low.

During that time, the practitioner was reading the best-selling *Jack: Straight from the Gut*. She was, of course, already familiar with Jack Welch's "be first or second, or get out of the market" strategy. But an unusual aspect of this idea resonated with her knowledge of her firm's business climate at that particular time.

It wasn't the content of Welch's strategy that made an impression on this idea practitioner; it was its conspicuous clarity. This leader knew she needed a strategic message that both was socializable in the organization and differentiated her firm from its competitors.

After the structural changes her firm had gone through, she and the CEO were crafting a new strategy. She knew they should do their best to harness the underlying power of the "one or two" strategy:

Since we've downsized, we've been trying to figure out how to energize the troops. When I was reading Jack, *I thought about his strategy statement in the context of what we do and had just gone through [emphasis added]. Jack's approach spoke to the "Who are we and what makes us special?" questions that were plaguing our firm. "One or two, or get out" sends a very clear message to employees about how you're making decisions, how the firm is making trade-offs, and where and how they should be devoting their energy. We focused on the fact that these times called for not just the right strategic message, but the right kind of messaging. And we will be consistent in how we promote the message; rather than trying to explain the strategy through a memo or press release, we will go on a road show to help socialize it internally and externally.*

We talked in detail about selling ideas in chapter 5. The important point here is that this idea practitioner translated Welch's ideas in terms of her organization's peculiar business climate and needs—the odd combination of its employees' moods after layoffs, and its position in the market relative to competitors. Welch's idea was translatable in her firm not as a strategy per se, but as a rallying cry.

Look for Good Timing

An idea cannot be a good fit unless it is also well timed. We believe the best way to develop a sense of timing is to frequently scan the zeitgeist—the economic, social, and political environment—in which an idea unfolds. What exactly do we mean by the zeitgeist? It is the complex interplay between economic, technological, political, and social forces—trade imbalances, globalization, deregulation policies associated with Republican administrations, the proliferation and fragmentation of the media from cable TV and the Internet—that can determine which ideas will flop and which ideas will fly. Journalists and other researchers have long understood that the success of a management idea often hinges on whether it is tapped into the zeitgeist (see sidebar). One study by a British researcher, for example, found that during the same time span, the rhetoric used to describe and promote Margaret Thatcher's economic policies was nearly indistinguishable from the rhetoric used by leading management gurus. Both described their projects "in cultural terms as necessary, and unavoidable missions to . . . reorient the economy and rekindle the spirit of enterprise."[1] Several other researchers have found strong correlations between the popularity of certain management ideas and economic indicators such as trade balance, consumer confidence, and unemployment rates.[2] As the U.S. trade deficit with Japan grew through the 1970s and 1980s, for example, management ideas became increasingly focused on quality.

There are two relevant issues here. As we just indicated, some ideas are just more in sync with the zeitgeist than others. Second, those who jump on an idea early by scanning the zeitgeist—say, before it goes into the program stage in your competitor's organization—often gain significantly more leverage than do late adopters. What's more, our research indicates a few tried and true ways to scan the zeitgeist to develop a sense of timing and even early mover advantage.

First, go to your local bookstore—physical or virtual—regularly and scan new business book titles and business magazine

The Zeitgeist: A Newsworthy Issue

Consider how each of the following four excerpts from management publications accounts for the relationship between the zeitgeist and a different management idea: customer relationship and supply chain management (CRM and SCM), deconstruction versus "blown to bits," work–life balance, and pay-for-performance.

1. **Technological Aspect (CRM and SCM)** Vendors often compete to capitalize on the interplay between zeitgeist shifts and management ideas: "The rise of customer relationship management (CRM) and supply chain management (SCM) technologies in the late 1990s shifted the battle to a new playing field, where SAP didn't have an easily established advantage. Upstarts like CRM pioneer Siebel Systems and supply chain specialist i2 Technologies got their feet in the doors of some big customers. Established rivals like Oracle and PeopleSoft sensed a new zeitgeist. . . . However, just a few years later, the business climate has shifted again."[3]

2. **Economic Aspect (Deconstruction/"Blown to Bits")** The impact of the late 1990s bull market and the Internet had a pronounced influence on the types of management ideas and the tenor of its rhetoric: "We must remember that 1991 through 2000—during which Philip Evans and Thomas S. Wurster researched and wrote *Blown to Bits*—were years of immense possibility in which thoughtful people were just as likely as those who were not to get caught up in the zeitgeist. Today, 'bubble' captures our longing and our regret for those brief but roaring years when all the fundamental suppositions of more than two centuries of economics and business were questioned and, truth be told, assumed by everyone other than the most curmudgeonly to have changed."[4]

3. **Social Aspect (Work–Life Balance)** New workplace demographics will often reshape long-held managerial assumptions

about where and how one should work: "The Zeitgeist, with its material consequences, molded organizational practices. For example, more generous parental-leave schemes and equal-opportunity initiatives were introduced in the banks. Balancing work and family life has become a question of individual solutions. . . . It is noteworthy that both our senior and branch-manager interviewees frequently made vague references to a changing 'atmosphere' in Finnish society in the 1980s and 1990s when explaining gender-related changes within the banks."[5]

4. **Remuneration Aspect (Pay-for-Performance)**   The zeitgeist often affects the way managers think about the best approaches to rewards and compensation: "I think the zeitgeist, if I can use that terrible term, of the times is definitely rewarding performance, performance focus, etc. That ties in to what we see as a continued growth of incentive plans and pay for performance."[6]

headlines. Ask the salesperson what's new and what's selling well, or check out a book's rank in sales figures on Amazon.com. Keep a running journal to track changes. Chris Hoenig, an idea practitioner and creator who has spent time in both the private and the public sectors, considers this scanning activity perhaps even more vital to his position than reading: "I read a lot. The [Wall Street] *Journal,* the [New York] *Times, MIT Technology Review,* and *Wired, Fortune,* and *Business Week.* But the most interesting ideas, I get in bookstores, just scanning the shelves. Just walk down the shelves. Look at the titles and the tables of contents. Look at what people writing books have to say—there's a layer of ideas in books that you don't find in magazines, that magazine journalists don't pick up on. Scanning requires that you be multidisciplinary—to look at both books and magazines."

As an important distribution channel of the publishing industry, bookstores evince the zeitgeist within which waves of activity and demand for particular management ideas rise and fall. When you notice three new books on outsourcing, when last month there were none, you know you're onto something. When you see six e-commerce strategy books in the bargain bin and note that there are no new ones, the conclusion is obvious. Jeffrey Krames, publisher and editor-in-chief of McGraw-Hill's trade division, sums up these factors: "Business publishers are not immune to [economic] cycles. . . . The dot-com game was about topline growth; the emphasis today is on the bottom line. Managers want long-term business models that work. Publishing programs reflect this zeitgeist."[7]

Another way to scan is to do keyword searches on good business databases like Factiva (www.factiva.com) or LexisNexis (www.nexis.com). As an example of this type of analysis, in 2002 one of us participated in a study on corporate venturing that was eventually picked up in the *Wall Street Journal*. We originally undertook the study to assess the correlation between corporate venturing in practice and its media coverage, which had soured, but not fallen off.

The rise of the wave was fairly typical. In 1995, one database registered seventeen keyword hits, then twenty-three the next year. In each of the following two years, there were just more than fifty hits. Then, between 1999 and 2001, the wave peaked to over two hundred hits, more than four times its 1998 height. During those peak years, however, the nature of the coverage changed from enthusiastic to sour. By the time our study was mentioned in the *Journal* in 2002, writers and experts were declaring corporate venturing dead. Of course, it will come back. The contrarian idea practitioner should be thinking now about the next wave of corporate venturing.

For these reasons, we need to be attentive to both the quantity and the tone of media coverage in assessing an idea. While tracking keyword hits may indicate upward or downward trends, a more detailed attention to rhetorical twists and turns is also required. Unless your organization is highly contrarian, one would be hard-pressed to try to introduce an idea to their organization—with or without its consultant or guru label—after the media sours on an idea. Even if the wave still seems to be cresting, you'd be paddling upstream.

Intense interest—even optimism—in the business press and heightened marketing and implementation efforts among the major management consultancies often mark the beginning of a wave's crest. Negative press coverage and burgeoning interest among academics often mark the start of a wave's recession. Savvy scanners seeking ideas on the downhill slope can supplement their searches of the business press by cross-checking titles and abstracts in academically oriented publications like *Management Science* or *Academy of Management Review*. Academics aren't typically early adopters or creators of new business ideas. And usually by the time an article makes it through the lengthy peer review—which often lasts more than a year—the wave is receding and it's too late to gain early mover advantage.

On the other hand, the home pages of major consulting firms evidence the final stages of a wave's rise and the first stages of its crest. A quick scan of their Web sites reveals each consultancy's brand of particular management idea. There's customer management strategy, CRM, balanced sourcing, supply-chain mastery, loyalty, and the war for talent. Consider this trifecta: creative destruction, transformational outsourcing, and profit from the core. Underlying each consultancy's rhetorical take is a single idea wave that heads in a particular direction, that is, wherever the zeitgeist is headed. Of course, sometimes all brands—and the idea itself—fail to follow the zeitgeist.

At first the zeitgeist seems like an elusive and unverifiable influence. But it can be studied and quantified. Idea practitioners can develop reliable scanning techniques. They can learn to track several ideas at once to find the best fit between an idea and their organization's current needs. It is worth emphasizing, however, that an idea practitioner should view the cycle of an idea in his or her particular organization as distinct from the overall cycle of the idea. We described this distinction between internal and external popularity of ideas in chapter 3. When scanning, idea practitioners should generally focus on ideas that mesh with the zeitgeist and are on the rise. Then, as we will describe in the next section, they should focus on whether the idea can be harmonized with the key themes in their organization's ongoing rhetoric.

Sometimes, of course, the internal zeitgeist dictates a conservative approach to business and management ideas. According to Lawrence Baxter, an idea practitioner and chief e-commerce officer of Wachovia Corporation, there are times to focus on new ideas and times when it's better to keep your head down and focus on the task at hand. Baxter is an inveterate idea practitioner (see sidebar). He realized, however, that when Wachovia and First Union agreed to merge, it wasn't a time to explore new business and management ideas: "We had a lot of very difficult and complex operational issues to address during the merger. There was a very clear focus on integrating the banks over a certain time period. It wasn't a time to explore new ideas that might add risk to the organization."

Baxter does feel that innovation was necessary during the merger, but it was directed to a different end: "The sheer pressure of integrating quickly forced us to generate and apply ideas for practical problem-solving." He hopes that even after the pressure subsides, the organizational climate will be more innovative. "Having to come up with tactical ideas during the merger may embolden some of our people to innovate strategically over the long term."

Another interesting aspect of timing in idea-based innovation, Baxter points out, is that the immediate needs of an event like a merger can lead to the application of long-known ideas:

In 1997 and 1998, I became intrigued by the idea of complex adaptive systems. I read some things, went to conferences, and thought the concepts were fascinating. The problem was that I could not see any real application of these ideas. For six years, complex adaptive systems stayed at the back of my mind. Now, during the merger, the wide-ranging stress-testing of Internet applications has become more critical. We often find that an application might appear to have plenty of capacity during tests, but when confronted with real customer usage, it breaks. All of a sudden it dawned on me that the basic problem is one of nonlinearity: Our extrapolations aren't predicting customer behavior well. Then I read an HBR article on agent-based modeling—a key technique in complex adaptive systems—and it seemed very promising. We're getting very interested in applying the technique for our testing, though we haven't actually done it yet. What is amazing to me, though, is the lag time between my hearing about the idea and actually understanding its real relevance.

Lawrence Baxter, Idea Practitioner

Lawrence Baxter spans not only intellectual domains, but also geographies. Born and raised in South Africa, he went on to England for additional legal education, ultimately ending up teaching regulatory law at Duke University's law school. Baxter developed a specialty in banking regulation. A member of the law school's board of visitors was also an executive at nearby Wachovia. He encouraged Baxter to join the bank as strategic counsel to advise the CFO on the business implications of banking reform legislation.

As an academic, Baxter had not studied technology, but he was an early adopter and active user. From 1981 to 1983, while still in South Africa, he wrote an entire legal treatise on one of the first so-called portable computers. Before departing Duke for Wachovia in 1995, he'd been a daily user of both Internet e-mail and the early versions of Web browsers. Since few at Wachovia were interested in Internet technology, he became an advocate. In 1996 he led a new emerging-businesses department and started an informal e-commerce group. This arrangement was formalized in 1997. Under the leadership of Baxter and some technology partnerships he cultivated, Wachovia became one of the early leaders in e-commerce among banks (First

Union, later to become Wachovia's merger partner, was already such a leader).

Baxter credits his youth in South Africa for his ability to thrive on change: "You could either turn a blind eye and just accept things as they are, with all their injustices and frustrations, or look for opportunities to change things." In both his academic and banking roles, he has sought out intellectual stimulation, challenge, and interesting work more than managerial responsibility. "I get bored about every seven years," Baxter says, "sort of a seven-year itch. Then I look for a completely new challenge." Since the late 1990s, he's become interested not only in the law, banking regulation, and e-business, but also in such diverse intellectual realms as interpretative theory and hermeneutics, contemporary particle physics, knowledge management, chaos and complexity theory, and many more.

In summary, to become an effective scanner, follow these suggestions:

- Take an experiential approach by visiting bookstores and libraries.

- Take a virtual approach by searching online bookstores, business databases, and consultancy Web sites.

- Determine how aggressive your organization wants to be in terms of the speed with which it adopts new ideas.

- Be proactive when you spot a wave that is rising and it seems like a good organizational fit.

- Keep good ideas that seem out of sync with the zeitgeist on the back burner—if an idea seems promising, but is not currently rising with the zeitgeist, it could be aligned someday. Ideas are cyclical. If a wave starts to rise, you'll be more poised than anyone to benefit from the upward momentum.

Harmonization

One doesn't have to be a musicologist or concert pianist to know the major musical keys. On your local classical FM station, for example, how many times have you heard the DJ announce, "Beethoven's Waldstein Sonata in C," or "Shostakovich's Symphony no. 10 in G"? Just as these keys are the foundation for musical variation from minor keys to major sevenths to flats, the key themes of innovation, effectiveness, and efficiency are the basis for almost all organizational idea-based change (as noted in chapter 3). And just as good musicians can hear the key of a composition with quick accuracy and improvise accordingly, idea practitioners need to listen for the key themes of their organization's discourse before they try to sell and implement an idea. Practitioners of this skill harmonize the key of an external idea with the key of an organization's internal rhetoric. Conversely, tone-deaf practitioners will try to introduce, say, an innovation-themed idea into an efficiency-focused organization.

In the Key of Efficiency

The charter of the Federal Aviation Administration (FAA) reads: "Safety and System Efficiency." Though the particular meaning of each of these prongs has changed enormously over the years—in light of technological and sociopolitical disruptions, like air-traffic controller strikes in the early 1980s and the September 11, 2001 disaster—the overwhelming focus of the organization is efficiency. Although the rhetoric of efficiency is a response to public demand and congressional mandate, the FAA has built the rhetoric into the way it does business. Consider what Giora Hadar, an idea practitioner and a proponent of knowledge and organizational learning at the FAA, says: "We are a conservative organization by nature, because we are responsible for promoting safety. We have regulations on how tight bolts on radars should be, for example. We emphasized TQM all along, before the quality movement. We don't 'produce' anything. Most everything we do is a joint venture with industry. We do the R&D, we develop the requirements, and then we hire contractors like Raytheon to actually produce the equipment we purchase."

Nevertheless, knowledge management (KM) was still not an easy sell, but Hadar developed a method of explaining KM to colleagues:

> *I pulled together a presentation and exhibit on how we could benefit from knowledge management. An engineer said to me over dinner, "I listened and looked through your KM stuff. To be honest with you, I don't see any way, shape, or form that we're going to be able to do it in the next three years. I have no use for it whatsoever." So, I thought to myself, I'm not going to argue over dinner with this guy. I asked him, "Alan, do me a favor. Describe to me what you've been doing for the last two years. How did you get to where you are, and what are you doing right now?" I spent two minutes listening to him as others at our table began to grin ear to ear. He looked at us, "Why are you grinning?" I said, "Alan, I hate to tell you this, but you're already doing knowledge management. You're just not calling it knowledge management."*

This was an important moment for Hadar's colleague, who has since then become a strong KM supporter. But it was even more pivotal for Hadar, who realized that selling is predicated on harmonizing preexisting discourse with the new one you intend to introduce—on building momentum from the words colleagues are already putting into action. He began the transformation from being a talker to a listener.

Ironically, he realized that the best way to reach a critical mass is to listen to critical individuals, that is, individuals who have initially negative responses to an idea. According to Hadar, they are the gatekeepers between widespread, internal resistance and strong advocacy.

Changing Keys: From Effectiveness to Innovation

When organizations change rhetorical keys—which often occurs as a result of CEO mandate—idea practitioners should change their focus as well. At Whirlpool, the key change in the late 1990s was global in scope. Demands from leadership, customers, and the capital markets instigated the change. Whirlpool had been a products company. But leadership was coming to the increasingly uncomfortable conclusion that products no longer drive loyalty. Brand and the total offer made to customers do. As Whirlpool shifted from a commodity product to a customer brand strategy, the company was shifting keys from being an efficiency-focused company to an innovation-focused one. And the senior leadership thought knowledge management could help make this innovation happen. According to Antonella Padova, an Italy-based manager, Whirlpool executives introduced the rhetoric of innovation to signal this major change of strategy: "Innovation came in because you cannot brand only a few products; you have to completely rethink the marketing process. Before, marketing was only focused on products. Now, product is just a piece of the equation. There's also communication, purchase process, service. . . . "

Long-standing industry terminology and financial goals were rethought, then renamed to reflect the new emphasis on innovation. The point is this: Rhetoric leads, and action follows. "Even our financial measurement changed. We now prefer it by 'brand result' instead of by product. It's difficult for a company—after ninety years—to rethink all processes, all systems, all tools, and all documents to a completely new focus. Even manufacturing, purchase, and procurement [now reflect the shift to innovation]."

Sure, strategy, processes, and structures were renamed. But Padova knew that if organizational and market realities were going to catch up to rhetorical changes, knowledge management would have to play a significant part. And the leadership agreed.

A global team was put together, and KM was attached to innovation. The goal was to support innovation teams. Seventy-five high-level people were assigned to design the innovation path for the company, to collect any ideas or contributions within the company, to develop those ideas into a business plan within a full and specific process to develop new businesses for the company. . . . The original impetus was to create an online environment that supported an offline innovation-focused culture. . . . 'Innovation E-Space' contains all the processes, tools, project and talent tracking systems to connect the right people. . . . Now, innovative ideas come in all forms and are gathered online—even simple ideas like, "Why don't we sell appliances as toys?"

But the point was not to capture ideas to build databases. The point was to build these ideas into innovative products and services. A one-hundred-day evaluation process was set up, and loan officers were brought in. Anyone, from blue-collar worker on the shop floor to a VP in a corner office, could join an innovation team to test his or her ideas. And KM enabled much of this process, especially the evaluation phase.

Marginalized Conversations as Evidence of Dominant Ones

Not everyone in an organization talks in the same key at the same time. Sometimes "marginalized" conversations spontaneously break out in alternative channels. Bulletin boards are filled with discussion threads that seek to gain the legitimacy and popularity through unofficial channels that they couldn't gain through organization-certified ones.

During 2001 and 2002, technology companies laid off tens of thousands of workers, sometimes using "efficiency" rhetoric. Web sites like www.vault.com hosted employee discussion boards that sought to expose these efforts as deleterious. With such crippled morale, many survivors exclaimed, how could we ever be as effective or innovative as we were before?

If anything, listening to these marginalized conversations can be an unlikely way for idea practitioners to accurately determine an organization's mainstream discourse. And since underground movements often anticipate aboveground ones, these marginalized discourses can often foretell the next set of conversations an organization will take—or needs to take. We recently saw this happen in a professional services firm, where the unofficial discourse offered an accurate forecast of the leadership's next two key changes.

Efficiency and Innovation in a Highly Decentralized Organization

Sometimes an organization can maintain two "official" discursive keys at once. As an idea practitioner, the trick is to modify the idea you intend to sell to your organization with the *right* discourse. When Dave Clarke was an executive at W. L. Gore, for example, the firm had at least forty businesses competing for resources, dollars, and people. Each business had its own market segments and commercializable ideas. All were using Gore's central chemical processing technology to meet these business needs. Gore was an innovation-driven organization, a very early mover (since 1958) in the corporate venturing movement. But this intense focus on innovation created its own set of problems: "Each business competed for venture capital. You can see the advantage of that immediately: It drives really quick response to a market need. The downside to this approach is that you can have the same problem solved six times over—and nobody would ever know it."

Clarke knew that KM was the best idea to address Gore's need to avoid duplication. In other words, the company needed to harmonize efficiency with innovation. But he also knew that the best way to introduce KM techniques was to build them on the rhetorical scaffolding of preexisting innovation initiatives. A talented listener, Clarke already knew that he wouldn't have to *push* KM; he could sell it across the organization from the pull side: "I don't think we talked about 'knowledge management'—I knew the phrase wouldn't resonate with people. What we talked about was global collaboration and global product development. We talked in terms of catch phrases. Like HP, we said, 'Let's make sure that Gore knows what Gore knows,' and 'Let's make sure we understand what "Gore Global" means.' I introduced and sold KM in the language that already resonated with people. In terms of the specific business need, we sold the idea that, 'Arizona needs to understand what Germany is doing, so we don't duplicate product efforts. Or, if [we] do, it better be for a good business reason.'"

Clarke's transitions between descriptions of organization reality—like specific business needs and the competitive landscape—and organizational rhetoric are both seamless and telling. "People at Gore didn't go around talking about 'taxonomies.' We didn't live in that world. The world we lived in was, 'We have an idea, and our job is to get that idea to market as quickly as possible.'" Clarke's point is straightforward. Organizations are their own conversational worlds. Listen and modify before you sell.

We don't intend to oversimplify. There is a vast array of organizational configurations. We talked to idea practitioners in high-tech and low-tech firms, in firms designed to sell "billions and billions" of hamburgers and in firms designed to sell financial advice, in perennial blue chips and in start-ups, in cowboy cultures and in hierarchical ones. One practitioner described his professional services firm as "a loosely organized confederation of franchises." Although we can apply the general principle that all firms are playing in one or, occasionally, more thematic keys—innovation, effectiveness, or efficiency—no two firms sound exactly alike. Idea practitioners who listen carefully and explicitly understand the key of their organizations are in a better position than anyone else to sell a new management idea in their firms.

Good listeners, of course, have ways of checking to ensure that they are listening well. Jim Kinney, a senior VP who introduced e-business to Kraft Foods, refers to this process simply as "testing ideas out through conversation." Other idea practitioners, like Mohi Ahmed at Fujitsu, describe this in terms of formal three-step process. After he has developed a "feel and sense for how the idea might work at Fujitsu," he discusses it with trusted sources. If it passes that checkpoint, he discusses it with a potential user. Only then will he begin dialogue with a potential executive sponsor. As the idea passes through each checkpoint, the likelihood increases that it could be smoothly introduced into the organization's broader discourse and successfully piloted.

Now That You've Found Your Ideas, Sell Them

An idea seems like a clean fit for your organization. Now what? Our research suggests that those who hope to successfully introduce, implement, and sustain ideas need to view themselves as salespeople (and sometimes brokers, as we mentioned in the previous chapter) in a marketplace of organizational ideas. In such a marketplace, there are considerations of scale, supply and demand, competition, value creation, and buyers and sellers.

Nowhere did we find a more sales-oriented approach to business improvement ideas than at Procter & Gamble, that temple of consumer marketing. Larry Huston, the R&D manager for innovation and knowledge, sees the time-honored principles of marketing and sales as applying just as well to breakthrough business ideas (what he calls idea products and organizational interventions) as to detergent. As Huston notes, there are many similarities: "Both deal with people. Both deal with selling something and influencing behavior. Both must address needs and emotions. And the same disciplined approach to understanding the needs, developing alternative stories and storyboards, and sensing the appeal of the different stories works just as well for ideas as it does products."

Huston has a basic process for addressing the early stages of business innovation. First, he seeks to understand the needs of two different customer groups: the end user of the idea, and management. He then develops several story options. The core elements of the stories are these:

- the promise
- the benefits and how they connect to features that deliver the benefits

- the reasons to believe in the promise and benefits

- the price (what you have to give to get the promise and benefits)

Several stories are then created in a storyboard format and massaged for insights; then key lessons are pulled out and a new "final story" is created. This final story is then refined until the "purchase intent" and believability objectives are met. Often, the reason to believe will come from highly credible sources involved in pilot or proof-of-concept efforts.

As with Procter & Gamble's approach to consumer products, Huston notes that this is a marketing-driven approach. Only when the firm creates a concept that has high appeal does it proceed to development and intervention activities.

Idea practitioners at other firms also employed various forms of marketing and sales approaches. Some of their methods are described by the particular objective of their efforts in the following sections.

Get Leadership on Board

Nearly all the idea practitioners we interviewed spoke of the unavoidable need to involve CEOs or other senior executives in some substantial manner during the internal selling process. Many spoke of the importance of taking the time-tested top-down, bottom-up approach. Sure, some practitioners, like Dave Barrow of BP, might view selling in terms of an iterative process, "a back and forth from CEO to the rank and file." But the power of the CEO to help your cause is at least equivalent to all other rank-and-file employees combined.

Ideally, you'll be able to wage a sales campaign both on the grassroots level and aimed at the CEO. But given the choice between dispersing one's limited time and attention widely or focusing on the CEO (or another senior executive sponsor with a budget), the answer should be clear. Of course, selling to only one individual can be risky. An idea practitioner who helped bring in the idea of reengineering at Xerox told us that he had substantial buy-in from the president of the U.S. division for his project. But then the president left the company. "We should have sold the idea to the entire executive team," he notes. With the sponsoring CEO gone, the project died.

Few people are as adept or experienced at selling new ideas to organizational leaders as Mitzi Wertheim, who works as a change consultant inside the largest corporate structure in the world, the Department of Defense. Where else are there more credentialed leaders? It is not insignificant that Wertheim comes from a long line of change agents, and her selling strategy is informed by this background. When her father worked at Bell Laboratories, he invented the push-button telephone and answering machine. Her mother, a pioneering child psychologist, is in *Ripley's Believe It or Not* for teaching babies how to roller-skate.

A social anthropologist by training, Wertheim's lineage is apparent in her creative approach to selling new ideas to organizational leaders: "I'm interested in the process of change—what enhances it and what impedes it. The question I ask is, What is it that is causing the dysfunctional behavior? When I understand that, the next question I ask is, What intervention would make a real difference?"

Wertheim's guiding questions are market savvy. First, she tries to understand where the demand—or "dysfunction"—is. Second, she seeks to understand which idea best meets this demand. She asks, Can this idea be sold in a way that actually meets demand?

Though some ideas took longer to sell than others, she has had notable success using this approach to sell ideas inside the Department of Defense. While she spent several years selling activity-based costing, she knew all along that it was the right idea to meet an acute demand. The Pentagon was, after all, emblematic of wastefulness and inadequate financial management. And a source of the dysfunction—"budgeting for an accounting system"—persisted. After a hard-fought sales campaign, one in which she focused on demonstrating demand to Pentagon brass, the secretary of the navy announced in 2001, "We're going to do activity-based costing."

Although we're talking about aligning supply with demand, idea with need, this need is rarely legitimized—in discourse or in financial action—until leadership says so. Wertheim learned this lesson quickly when she was working for a huge multinational corporation in the private sector and proposed what she believed to be a strong idea to a senior VP. He liked the idea as well. "But," he said, "we've already selected our metric, and our metric is speed." Her conclusion: "If the suggestion that you make doesn't fit onto the plate that leadership is looking at, at that moment, they don't focus on it."

Since then, Wertheim has honed a formidable sales strategy, one geared toward selling to leaders. In an organization as large, complex, and rank-focused as the Department of Defense, however, there are plenty of leaders. Here are the nuts and bolts of her sales approach (and since she picked these up at the Pentagon, they're worth plenty!):

- Understand the incentives for change—where the demand lies—and aim your sales toward these.

- Know who is going to pay for the initiative and why they should pay for it.

- Put ideas inside what is already in leadership's focus.

- Don't sell a technology.

- Go on a "book tour," promoting and "signing the inside jacket" of the idea in person.

- Don't hit your head against a brick wall. If one organizational leader isn't interested in the idea, then find one who is—enroll him or her as your sponsor.

- Build a base of support, and work with a group of people who say, "This makes sense."

Of course, sometimes the best sales strategy won't work. Another important issue in working with leaders on new ideas is knowing when to give up and move along. For example, Valerie

Norton, an idea practitioner who now works at the financial services firm ING Barings Group, once attempted to introduce some sophisticated organizational learning ideas at her previous place of employment, a telecommunications firm. She explains that she had no success: "It just wasn't working. They weren't ready for these ideas at all—they were focused on much more basic issues of organizational survival. In terms of Maslow's hierarchy of needs, I was preaching about self-actualization, and they were living in the land of food, clothing, and shelter."

Seed, Select, and Amplify

The preceding discussion is only a broad sketch of how to begin a sales campaign in an organizational market. What are the particular market dynamics that idea practitioners should be aware of? What specific steps must idea practitioners take to attune their sales approach to these conditions? In spite of the striking variety and differences between organizations, all successful sales campaigns should be built on three prongs: seed, select, and amplify. These terms come from the field of cybernetics. The first refers to implementation; the second to creating and scaling the idea around demand; the third to demonstrating ongoing value.

Seed and Select

It is usually not a good idea to try to implement a new idea using an all-or-nothing approach. Although revolutionary proclamations may suggest otherwise, significant change takes time. Remember all that you-can-reengineer-your-corporation-in-a-year rhetoric? Nearly every organization that tried to accomplish that feat would have been better off taking the long view and beginning the reengineering journey with experiments. This is confirmed in both our research and our personal experience—though we have been advocating this approach all along. (In *Process Innovation,* one of us [TD] said organizations should take a five-year view.)[8]

Successful implementation is therefore almost always predicated on seeding ideas in an organization through experiments. Experimentation allows idea practitioners to test demand and to modify the idea to organizational idiosyncrasies while also mitigating financial risks. It allows them to gauge fit, potential strengths, and weaknesses. One idea practitioner outlines the experimentation stage in terms of creating a benevolent virus:

- Design the virus's genetic makeup by making it appealing and self-propagating.

- Build a small application of the idea, showing people that it can work. But also make sure people know the idea can be rejected.

- When it gets to the point at which a decision needs to be made on broad implementation, decide whether you want to continue your efforts to push it over that threshold or whether it should be rejected. This is the select stage of the process.

- Since you have created an atmosphere of constant idea creation, focus on the ideas that are being accepted and replicated—and don't worry about the others.

We have already discussed the importance of selling an idea in light of the ongoing discourse or discourses of an organization. Before implementing a new idea, an idea practitioner has to decide whether to label it. Do you use the exact name that the guru uses in his or her book or in the *Harvard Business Review* article? "Hey folks, why don't we start a Swarm Intelligence pilot program?" Or, "We need to start cultivating some leaders around here. Let's try Bennis's new Crucibles idea!"

For some organizations, this approach will work. But often the best approach is to introduce the idea in your organization's own language in terms of new and ongoing concerns. Chris Hoenig successfully introduced best practices into the IT function at the General Accounting Office. His initial concern was to "align the points that have the highest receptivity with the points that have the highest need." But selling this alignment—that business might be better by trying this idea—requires some rhetorical sophistication. Here's a lesson he took away from this and later selling experiences:

> *Labeling is important. Some organizations are receptive to ideas with labels. They're generally very tolerant of labeled ideas as long as they're explained well. Here, labeled ideas will be taken seriously depending on whether they are good or not. Other organizations are not used to or do not have a high currency of ideas, and therefore, you cannot label them when you're trying to initially sell. Period. Instead, you should use the language of problems the organization is facing. Know the type of organizational culture you're talking to, which approach they'll listen to. The next stage of determining the label is based on whether the organization likes to try new things. Some are more receptive to ideas that are more scientific, others more practical, those suggesting that the organization can work faster. Others have a high tolerance for creative and design-oriented work, or longer cycle times.*

Reuben Slone, a VP of North America supply chain at Whirlpool, doesn't believe that his organization has much tolerance for labels. An early contributor and expert in reengineering, Slone has worked with several other brand-name ideas as well, but he doesn't introduce ideas by their brand name. He tinkers, makes adjustments, and introduces ideas around actual operational problems.

Like most idea practitioners, he's an avid and multidisciplinary reader. He doesn't just want to know what the emerging and powerful ideas in business are; he wants to know what makes them such. For this reason, he regularly reads books about complexity theory and has been a subscriber to *The Systems Thinker*. For a timeless perspective, he reads classics by seasoned thinkers like Chris Argyris, Russ Ackoff, and Peter Drucker. But he also scans for breaking ideas in *Fortune*, the *Wall Street Journal*, and *Harvard Business Review*.

He is a no-nonsense synthesizer of ideas. Through experimentation, he puts these ideas into play, then scales them up across the operational practice. Disinclined to introduce new ideas using guru labels, he instead labels ideas in terms of a specific business problem. To do this requires that he regularly applies rubber to asphalt: The best way to match a good idea with a real problem is not only to read about the front lines, but also to visit them. Experimentation, like scanning, requires a free play between intellect and experience. "Diversity of intellectual diet is so critical," says Slone. "But this entails not just reading. I just spent two days at our warehouse facilities in Ohio—Clyde, Findlay, Marion. There were practices I saw in one facility that just weren't applicable in another facility, but led me to think of ways in which we could just change them slightly to make them applicable to our entire business."

The factory distribution centers in Whirlpool's Marion facility are colocated with their factories. Each building is connected by a long conveyor, over a mile long, on which washers and dryers travel throughout the day. The original facility designers theorized that there should be a distinct separation between the production plant and the warehouse. But this separation came to embody how management in each building communicated.

The plant may change its production sequence on any given day because of part shortages or supplier issues. As a result, the plant may be building something different from what was in the original schedule. The master scheduler would then make those changes accordingly, but he wouldn't communicate them to the order coordinator at the distribution center. The plant would start building something different—a different-sized dryer, say— and wouldn't inform distribution, which would be waiting with the wrong-sized boxes, resources, and other distribution strategies.

As Slone tells it, this problem was fundamentally social. Trust, collegial networks, and an experiential understanding of how the other building operated were never established. In fact, the industrial engineers designed the barrier intentionally years back. Slone then started a small initiative to facilitate the exchange of social capital between the two buildings. Simple strategies, like including phone calls and visits in calendars. These strategies were initially aimed at improving collaboration to address an issue specific to that plant, but are now being scaled across the operation organization, from supply chain to manufacturing to product development:

> *It became apparent there were several of these opportunities [to improve collaboration]. For example, our production planners that schedule all our plans talk daily to the master scheduler in the plants, but they never visit the plant. Conversely, the master scheduler never visits corporate. [From the initial experiment], we realized there was a much greater need to walk in the other guy's shoes. So we very quickly got a message out to all our plants that our order coordinators should talk several times a day to make sure we're synchronizing the staging of equipment and people to any kind of variation at all that may occur in the daily production schedule. Then we realized we could broaden it even further. We had similar issues between our production planners and master schedulers in the plant, and it certainly would make some sense to have the production planners, with some frequency, visit the plants they're scheduling, which they typically never do. We then built this approach out to the deployment planners, who schedule the resourcing at the regional distribution centers, which are—in essence—the places where the customer interaction occurs with the trade. At this stage it was about shifting the focus from computer screens and pieces of paper to the people and equipment executing this—getting [the deployment planners] to understand the particulars of what can and can't work.*

In an age of highly automated and transparent supply chains, one would expect technology to have already rooted out some of the inefficiencies that Slone mentions. But Whirlpool didn't need a whiz-bang technology; it needed a managerial innovation—albeit a simple one.

Earlier we noted that Whirlpool was innovating in product and services. By introducing real social change in the operational side of the business, Slone is carrying Whirlpool's "innovation" mantra into unexpected places. He gained support and buy-in from senior leadership throughout the process, never labeling the initiative as anything other than an opportunity to "communicate better" and "drive mutual adjustment."

Amplify

There is a multiplicity of ways to detect latent and conspicuous demand, experiment around that demand, and then scale the idea up. Where should one focus these efforts? Susan Conway, an idea practitioner at Microsoft currently focused on measuring and improving the productivity of information workers, suggests determining your company's core businesses and focusing experiments around those: "Is Microsoft an innovator and on the cutting edge in everything we do? No, but we are [cutting edge] with software or technology around intellectual capital. We are so heavily invested in these that ideas should and do surround them. But there aren't many ideas around manufacturing techniques and things of that nature."

Here Conway suggests that idea practitioners ask themselves the question "Where and how is value created in my firm?" She says that ideas should not be introduced indiscriminately in any department, process, or function in your firm (though the dynamism that ideas can arouse is generally a good thing). Ideas should be focused and sold around a firm's value centers.

At the pharmaceutical firm Bristol-Myers Squibb, for example, R&D is a primary value center, but marketing is another one. Carol Bekar, an idea practitioner overseeing information initiatives, has been very deliberate throughout her career in her approach to introducing and managing the idea sales process. Her current challenge is how to scale the idea around the firm's other value center without dispersing her resources and budget too widely: "About two years ago, we were completely in the R&D

organization. We have an umbilical cord to intellectual property protection and a robust patenting service, for example. . . . So [now] my concern is how do we leverage what we've done for R&D into marketing without draining resources and making us ineffective across the board."

Interestingly, this is the price idea practitioners pay for their success. Thanks to Bekar's efforts, leadership saw the value of information management in R&D and wanted it expanded across the firm. Here it might be helpful to work backward a bit. Bekar has waged a classic sales campaign. She helped introduce information management into the ongoing thematic stream of the organization. She worked with leadership or, in her words, "found a champion." She built relationships, trust, and networks inside and outside the organization. She started small and labeled early initiatives in terms that addressed real business problems in familiar language. (She aligned and labeled the initiative with already established "informatics" initiatives). She managed expectations along the way.

But she was also deliberate about what she calls "demonstrating value for metrics." In the pharmaceutical industry, where the name of the game is the blockbuster drug, the metric of information management is often speed. Here's how she describes one initiative: "At one time I had the compound distribution group in my area, and I moved forward with proposing and buying a robotic, automated, compound store-and-retrieve system. It cost millions. The business value was to enable high throughput screening, a new process to identify more drug candidates more rapidly. [We were demonstrating value by enabling R&D] to do things faster and smarter."

While tying ideas into an organization's value centers should be a staple of an idea practitioner's sales repertoire, most consider it vital to demonstrate value on multiple fronts. The goal here is to amplify the legitimacy and the cognitive authority of the idea around the organization. It's about signaling value in indirect ways. Our research suggests that idea practitioners should also achieve the following:

- Find ways to link idea creation and implementation to merit—allow ideas to build reputations and careers. Create job titles and responsibilities around the idea. We believe, for example, that we were the first to talk and write about the so-called chief knowledge officer (CKO) role. This helped to create some tangible activity around the area of knowledge management and to institutionalize it within firms.[9]

- Link ideas to clients and customers. For example, "In the six months since we started the CRM initiative, we became 55 percent more effective at responding to customer needs, realizing a 12 percent jump in sales."

- Locate, substantiate, and then broadcast exemplary numbers in interoffice newsletters and to journalists (at least when you really want to grab investor or CEO attention) to demonstrate payback, return on investment, and organizational dynamism. These numbers have the meme-like ability to replicate themselves and to create buzz inside and outside an organization. For example, "Since we ramped up our corporate venturing initiatives earlier this year, we've brought twelve new technologies to market, eleven more than last year."

- Broadcast early wins using stories and other narrative techniques. A good story will sell itself. Speaking of his own narrative technique, one idea practitioner said, "Get the metaphor right. More than anything, these can build up cultural momentum."

Demonstrating and broadcasting the value of an idea is a fundamentally social activity. It's about building trust, enthusiasm, and a sense of ownership. Idea practitioners must know how to appeal to both goodwill and rational self-interest. Throughout the sales process, the idea and the salesperson are indistinguishable. "There's a critical mass of capabilities for an ideas person focused on selling," says Hoenig, "earnestness, credibility, passion—and the kind of directional sense that can inspire discipleship." Ironically, when it comes to ideas, social ability is equally as important as intellectual ability.

Amplification is also about building scale. It's relatively easy to staff up for a pilot, or even a single, project. But by the time an organization treats an idea as a program, it's difficult to work on the new idea as well as the existing business. At this point it's common for firms to seek outside help from consultants or other advisers. Unless the idea is completely and radically new, it's likely that at least one outside firm will have developed a practice area around it. That in itself can add credibility to an idea.

In chapters 1 through 4, we described the key resources of idea-based change: the idea practitioners, the gurus, and the ideas themselves. Chapter 5 and this chapter have discussed how effective idea practitioners can take an idea from the external market to a supported reality within their organizations. Chapters 7 and 8 will shift to a bit of ethnography—detailed accounts of how two popular ideas took flight (and sometimes crashed) within organizations. Since we were there for both events, we'll be describing them as participants and observers—a common practice among anthropologists.

7

THE REENGINEERING TSUNAMI

A CASE STORY OF AN IDEA
THAT BECAME A TIDAL WAVE

I<small>N THIS CHAPTER</small>, we'll describe the history of one particular business idea: business process reengineering. A detailed examination of one particular big idea will help idea practitioners distinguish good ideas from bad, useful selling approaches from useless ones, and positive movements based on ideas from nonproductive, hype-laden ones. These lessons make it worth dredging up the past and focusing again on a topic that many people blame for the loss of their jobs, and that many hold up as the poster child of management faddism. Reengineering is not an ideal example of how to surf the wave of new ideas. It is, however, an object lesson in how to avoid being crushed by a short-lived but powerful intellectual tsunami. There is also some evidence that reengineering is coming back as an idea—and it should, because aspects of it are timeless. We hope that this chapter will help idea practitioners deal with not just the past of reengineering, but also its future.

Reengineering is also of personal interest to at least one of us. With his coauthor Jim Short of MIT, Tom is generally credited with writing the first (by a few weeks) substantial article on reengineering, though not the most popular one.[1] He then wrote the first book on the subject—though again not the most popular one.[2] Tom's experiences in pushing a relatively moderate, academically rigorous, and popular-but-not-wildly-so version of the subject may be very instructive to any idea practitioner attempting to distribute big ideas in conservative clothing. Though Larry and Jim weren't heavily involved in the reengineering movement, we'll stick with the term "we" when we describe our own roles just to remain consistent with the rest of the book.

At its height, business process reengineering was one of the biggest business ideas ever. Business historians of the future will characterize the 1990s as the decade of reengineering. Described in more than twenty-five books (one of which—not Tom's, unfortunately—sold over two million copies) that were translated into multiple languages, featured in articles in every major business publication, discussed at hundreds of conferences, reengineering penetrated every continent with the possible exception of Antarctica.

Reengineering became a money machine for several of its constituents: the gurus who propounded the idea (at least a couple of them!), the consulting firms that offered reengineering services to their clients, and the computer and software vendors who managed to convince firms that their wares were critical to successful reengineering. Unfortunately, the idea did not enrich those who were most responsible for its birth and continued life within organizations: our faithful idea practitioners. Although these individuals played their customary heroic roles on the reengineering stage, others generally got all the credit. We'll try to redirect some of this credit to them in this chapter.

What Was and Is Reengineering?

Reengineering today means different things to different people. In the early writings on reengineering, however, there was substantial consensus on the definition. In the "classical" view, reengineering incorporated several different ideas:

- the radical redesign and improvement of work

- the attacking of broad, cross-functional business processes

- "stretch" goals of order-of-magnitude improvement

- the use of IT as an enabler of new ways of working

Among the general business audience, however, other meanings of the term proliferated. To some, reengineering came to mean any attempt within organizations to change how work is done—even incremental change of small, subfunctional processes. To others, it became a code word for downsizing. The latter meaning wasn't really fair, since none of the original literature on reengineering had stressed that objective. It was a somewhat cynical adoption of the word by senior executives (and their communications staffs) that brought this meaning into being.

We still remember the first time the reengineering-as-cutting-heads meaning appeared in the press. Around 1995, Pacific Bell announced that it was cutting ten thousand employees. Because of "reengineering," it didn't need them anymore, the press release said. We were conducting some research at Pac Bell at the time, and we knew that although the company was doing some reengineering, it certainly was not far enough along for anyone to know how many people (if any) would be freed up. The primary objectives of the major reengineering initiative at Pac Bell involved provisioning new telephone service faster and more accurately, not downsizing. Shortly thereafter, Apple Computer announced a similar reduction using the "r word." We were also familiar enough with that company to know that it wasn't true reengineering.

What happened to the term *reengineering* is typical of the proliferation of meanings that accompanies any successful new business idea. Consultants, middle and senior managers, and

FIGURE 7 - 1

Reengineering in the P Cycle

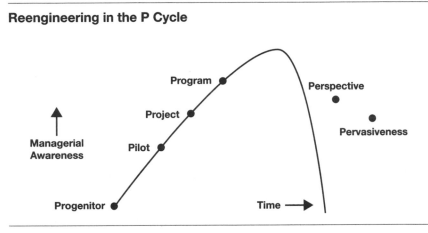

vendors had lots of incentives to jump on the reengineering band-wagon. Experts in continuous improvement, systems analysis, industrial engineering, and cycle time reduction all suddenly became experts in reengineering. We once heard a senior staffer from the California legislature say at a Harvard Kennedy School of Government conference that reengineering was "any project I want to get funded." Of course, saying that all these diverse activities were forms of reengineering raised expectations for the term, and no doubt hastened its demise. The late adopters of the term for their own purposes dropped it rapidly as soon as it became unpopular.

In terms of the P cycle (from pilot to project, program, perspective, and, finally, pervasiveness stages) we've described in chapter 3 as ideal for business ideas, reengineering doesn't have an ideal trajectory (figure 7-1). It rose too fast through the project and program levels and declined just as quickly when disillusionment and dashed expectations set in. Reengineering never made it beyond the program stage to a broad perspective or pervasiveness in most organizations. In the rest of the chapter, we'll describe why reengineering took on this unhealthy curve.

Why Was Reengineering So Popular?

We can only speculate as to why reengineering became such a popular movement. Most important, perhaps, were the zeitgeist factors. In the early 1990s, when reengineering was broadly adopted, an economic recession was under way. Companies needed to cut costs, and reengineering offered a more respectable-sounding approach than simply cutting heads. Even though the recession ended in the U.S. in 1993, however, reengineering remained popular for several years thereafter. Consequently, this economic explanation can be only partially correct.

As we've noted, business ideas tend to swing back and forth between a focus on what business to be in—innovation and competitive positioning—versus how to do the business—efficiency and productivity. The decade prior to reengineering featured a heavy focus on strategy and competition. Harvard professor Michael Porter's books on competitive strategy and differentiation were popular during the 1980s. Articles on IT in business focused on how these tools changed the way companies could compete. Perhaps by 1990 the business world was ready for a focus on how to do work faster and more efficiently. Indeed, the popular book *Competing Against Time,* published in 1990, presaged the idea of redesigning processes to save time.[3]

The 1990s were also the decade in which IT entered organizations in a highly visible way. Personal computers, introduced during the early 1980s, became much less expensive and much more popular. The Internet began to be used in business (though not substantially until the middle and late 1990s). Enterprise systems packages, which provided IT support for the same broad, cross-functional business processes that reengineering initiatives purported to redesign, also became broadly available during the decade. All the developments in IT surely drove managers to try to find new ways to use the technology to business advantage and improved productivity.

One could also argue that reengineering offered itself up to managers at a time when several long-term trends had reached critical mass. Perhaps the concept was taken up, for example, when many organizations were ready to respond to global competition and more demanding customers. Paul Strassman has argued that reengineering's popularity derived from the increasing proportion of white-collar workers in organizations.[4] Many reengineering initiatives addressed such white-collar processes as customer service and order management.

Finally, it is possible that reengineering became popular because of the activities of its proponents. Certainly Michael Hammer's 1990 *Harvard Business Review* article on reengineering ("Don't Automate, Obliterate") captured the excitement and imagination of many managers. The article and the subsequent book Hammer coauthored with Jim Champy—*Reengineering the Corporation*—was full of revolutionary fervor. These two sources made reengineering look both appealing and easy. Hammer also engaged many followers in his regular "Hammer Forums," conferences devoted to reengineering topics.

In addition to Hammer's activities, consultants at Index Group, which had an ongoing collaboration with Hammer, and at Ernst & Young, where we worked as researchers, began to publicize the concepts of reengineering in print and speaking engagements. Shortly thereafter, when it became apparent that there were willing clients and big dollars associated with reengineering consulting engagements, many other consulting firms began to jump on the idea. After that, vendors of software and hardware began to argue—in advertisements and presentations to potential customers—that their products were particularly conducive to reengineering. We called the combination of top managers wanting a new approach, management consultants, and IT vendors *the reengineering industrial complex;* together, these groups constituted a powerful force.[5]

Was Reengineering New?

Since one of the focal points in this book is the novelty of new business ideas, the question arises, "Was reengineering a new idea?" Certainly its partisans would have you think so. On the cover of the best-seller *Reengineering the Corporation,* Peter Drucker writes, "Reengineering is new, and it must be done." And Hammer refers to himself as the originator of reengineering, which suggests that the idea didn't exist before him.

Chalk a lot of this newness up to self-promotion and hype. Certainly Drucker, whose historical sense is far better than ours, should know that all the pieces of reengineering were present well before 1990. However, these components had not previously been brought together as one management concept. So if reengineering was new, it was only as a new synthesis of previously existing ideas.

The idea of managing and improving business processes came primarily from the quality and continuous-process-improvement movements, which themselves date back to Frederick Taylor and industrial engineering at the beginning of the twentieth century. Working on broad, cross-functional processes is more recent, but is certainly inherent in Porter's value chains from the early 1980s and in the design-for-manufacturing concept that became popular in the late 1980s.

Another key idea in reengineering was to start with a "clean sheet of paper" in the redesign of processes. This idea also wasn't new, having been explored in the largely synonymous greenfield approach to work design that was somewhat popular in the 1970s. And in textbooks of the 1950s and 1960s, we found references to using IT as a way to change work.

In our publications on reengineering, we tried to make clear that reengineering had its roots in these preexisting ideas. But this was probably a big commercial mistake, even if undeniably true. Most managers would like to believe that they are employing an entirely new concept, not a riff on old scores.

How Did the Idea Come About?

As with most of the business ideas discussed in this book, the real creators of reengineering weren't consultants or academics. They were businesspeople—middle managers, mostly—who needed to serve their customers better and solve their vexing business problems. These idea practitioners often began to practice some form of reengineering in their own work and to refine the concepts in their work with consultants and academics. But there were still handsome rewards for those who could name, codify, and popularize what these innovative managers were doing.

In the late 1980s and early 1990s, well before anyone had written articles or books on the subject, the idea of reengineering was in the air, waiting for someone to grab it. At the Index Group, a Cambridge, Massachusetts, consulting firm where Tom worked as director of research (the company later became CSC Index), a smart and well-liked senior consultant named Gary Gulden and others talked about how to improve management processes or how to "blow up the warehouse" in logistical processes. (The blow-up metaphor was coined by Dave Robinson, another Index Group executive.) Hammer, whose office was a couple of floors down from ours, had been an MIT professor and an office-automation expert. In that now-dead field, he argued that it made sense to re-design office procedures before bringing in such then-advanced technologies as word processing—a primitive form of the re-engineering idea. Other consulting firms, including our big rivals Nolan, Norton & Co. (later acquired by KPMG, and founded in part by Dave Norton, who eventually became a popularizer of the balanced scorecard) and the Boston Consulting Group, were talking and writing about the same notions, though not very visibly. This heady mixture of gaseous ideas was only waiting for a spark, but it had to come at the right time. In 1988 we proposed an article on the subject (which probably would have been coauthored by Hammer, since we were working closely together) to the editors at the *Harvard Business Review*, but they turned it down. Perhaps they were wise in doing so, because the concept then lacked sufficient depth and examples.

The necessary field work came from a research project within PRISM (Partnership for Research in Information Systems Management), a multiclient research program that was a joint venture of Index Group and Hammer. As we've noted in previous chapters, such multiclient programs are a good way to bring together practitioners of new ideas—real businesspeople with real problems—with people like Hammer and us, who like to refine and write about these ideas.

The particular research project that gave reengineering a boost was called Managing Cross-Functional Systems. This project uncovered several interesting stories about companies that were using IT to redesign cross-functional processes. One of these, for example, was Mutual Benefit Life Insurance, a Newark, New Jersey, company that had radically redesigned the way it issued insurance policies. The key idea practitioners, Keith Glover (senior VP of individual insurance administration) and Chuck McCaig (senior VP of corporate services), concluded that powerful personal computers would make it possible for one case manager to take on the entire process of issuing an insurance policy. Glover, McCaig, and the other managers and workers at Mutual Benefit radically improved the time required to issue a policy, but some of the power of their example was drained away when the company's investment portfolio led it into receivership.

Another early example of reengineering that PRISM researchers found was at Hewlett-Packard. The process by which this happened illustrates nicely the symbiotic relationship between the managers who create new business ideas and the gurus who cogitate on and write about them. Charles "Chuck" Sieloff, then a senior IT manager at HP, is one of our prototypical idea practitioners (see sidebar). Sieloff was one of the sponsors of PRISM and alerted the research team on cross-functional systems to a project at HP that seemed to have all the characteristics we were seeking. It centered around a radical change in how goods and services were purchased at HP. Prior to this application, each HP business unit purchased things according to its own needs and processes. This ensured that the unit got what it wanted, but it didn't allow for any volume discounts with suppliers or any centralized management of what was bought.

Chuck Sieloff, Idea Practitioner

Charles "Chuck" Sieloff was an idea practitioner at Hewlett-Packard for twenty-eight years. He's a thoughtful, bright man with a Ph.D. in European history from Stanford University. After getting his degree, he found that there were few jobs in European history, and many in IT. He consequently moved in the IT direction and stayed in the field throughout his career. A broad thinker for an IT person, however, he works on such topics as organizational change management, quality, knowledge management, and the management of attention, in addition to reengineering. Sieloff's role at HP was to bring in some very important ideas to the company, several of which took root and flourished. His quiet, cooperative, and patient manner undoubtedly contributed to his success—particularly in an environment like HP's, where he was someone from "corporate" in a company with a culture of divisional autonomy. He never seemed to care that his own involvement was visible—only that the company benefited from the ideas and the work with external thinkers. HP repaid his favors by being a great company and treating Sieloff and other employees very well. Now retired from HP, Sieloff works part-time as a researcher at the Institute for the Future, a Silicon Valley think tank. His job there illustrates the fine line between gurus who propagate ideas and the managers who implement them.

A new executive, Gordon Olson, was brought in from the automobile industry to serve as the head of corporate materials, a new position for HP that included logistics, distribution, and procurement. Work soon began on a system and new process that would support a common procurement process for all of HP's business units, while still allowing the business units to initiate purchases. For the first time, HP would be able to develop a consolidated forecast of the goods to be purchased, and the company could employ a common purchase order, contracts, and approach to vendor relationships. Sicloff was the IT person on the project, but was also a full partner on the business team leading the change.

The new system and process, unlike many other reengineering efforts, was completely successful, saving HP hundreds of millions of procurement dollars over its ten-year life span. But like other reengineering projects, it created substantial political controversy, and Olson and Sieloff had to spend an enormous amount of time persuading the business units to use the system.

When Sieloff observed from the PRISM study that other companies were pursuing similar "reengineering" projects, he became interested in how HP could attempt to institutionalize this type of change. He paid close attention to the PRISM results and to other writing on reengineering by the early gurus. Well after the procurement process had been reengineered, he enlisted internal collaborators. Sieloff knew that other groups within HP had interest in the general topic of process change and work redesign. One, called Workplace Effectiveness (led by another thoughtful manager, named Stu Winby) had a history of collaborating with the IT function. There were other related movements in the air at the same time; the Workplace Effectiveness group, for example, was enamored of a movement that sought to manage the so-called white space within organizations, or the spaces between positions on the organization chart. This movement was advocated by Geary Rummler and Alan Brache, two other consultants. Sieloff and Winby agreed to collaborate on a series of educational events for HP business units that would help them understand how to undertake both reengineering and white-space projects. External consultants delivered the education, but the HP managers made sure that their messages were consistent with HP's philosophy of process and organizational change and with the organizational culture.

For this reason, Sieloff at HP and McCaig and Glover at Mutual Benefit Life are among the true heroes of reengineering. The gurus get the credit and the book sales and the podium appearances, but reengineering was invented by these middle managers and then made real. There are many other examples of these innovators, some of whom appeared in the early accounts of reengineering. Hammer and Champy's *Reengineering the Corporation,* for example, tells of Regis Filtz at Bell Atlantic, Pam Godwin at the Direct Response Group of Capital Holding, and Robert Stark of Hallmark Cards.[6] Hammer and Champy were generous in crediting these adventurous managers. Many early adopters of reengineering, of course, were never known to the public.

Where Did Reengineering Go Astray?

Like any other business idea, reengineering had to be bought by companies and sold, most often by business gurus. The failure of reengineering to go the full cycle of a business idea can be attributed to both parties during its transfer and implementation.

Guru Shortcomings

In late 1996, a front-page *Wall Street Journal* article featured a confession by Hammer: "Dr. Hammer points out a flaw: He and the other leaders of the $4.7 billion re-engineering industry forgot about people. 'I wasn't smart enough about that,' he says. 'I was reflecting my engineering background and was insufficiently appreciative of the human dimension. I've learned that's critical.'"[7]

This issue was most prominently manifested in Hammer's rhetoric, which was characterized in an article by Paul Strassman as "extremist." Hammer used such phrases as "in reengineering we carry the wounded and shoot the stragglers," "On this journey we shoot the dissenters," and "It's basically taking an ax and a machine gun to your existing organization."[8] The nature of this rhetoric not only made employees who were reengineering their companies fear for their livelihoods; it also raised expectations of managers for revolutionary changes that couldn't really be delivered.

There is little doubt that the Hammer and Champy version of reengineering was guilty of overblown rhetoric in general (most of this rhetoric comes either from Hammer or from ghostwriters; Champy is more genial and mild-mannered). Both in Hammer's 1990 *Harvard Business Review* article and in Hammer and Champy's 1993 book, the claims were extravagant and unsupported by fact. The book cover suggests, for example, that "Everything you thought you knew about business is wrong," and highly simplistic arguments are made throughout. The book itself also suggests that prior to the golden age of reengineering, customers were placid and undemanding, but now (as of 1993) they know exactly what they want and will not be deterred from getting it. In the past, business was static, but now it is a realm of constant change. Business processes are angelic; business functions, demonic. The rhetoric has been described as theological, "not because they speak of a recognizable deity, but because they seek to provide a means to situate, and to explain America's corporate slippage (the fall) whilst, simultaneously, spelling out the steps which must be taken to ensure corporate America's salvation."[9]

As the use of the word *whilst* in the quotation suggests, the author of the foregoing critique of reengineering is English. For some reason the English have delighted in criticizing reengineering and managerial gurus in general.[10] Perhaps the rhetoric frequently associated with new business ideas is incompatible with the stereotypical British reserve. But the critics seem to miss the point of all this rhetoric. If management writers don't get the attention of readers and managers, their work will have no influence. Unfortunately, the critics always seize upon the worst examples of guruistic rhetoric, rather than addressing more moderate authors and speakers.

The greatest shortcoming of the Hammer and Champy reengineering work is not that it neglects people or that it employs overblown rhetoric, but that it fails to acknowledge how difficult, time-consuming, and expensive it is to reengineer. They implied that one could reengineer an entire corporation—the title of the book was, after all, *Reengineering the Corporation*—in as little as a year. We are not suggesting that Hammer and Champy intentionally misled anyone; they're both honorable men. This unfounded optimism was, however, a major factor in the rapid rise and fall of reengineering. Inspired by reading the book, managers initiated projects in their own companies with high expectations of rapid success. But when they encountered difficulties and slipping project deadlines, many became disenchanted and dropped their projects. This inability of reengineering to live up to its expectations is the primary reason why its P cycle was so dysfunctional and ineffective.

While we're on the subject of confession, we'll make one of our own. With two chapters on the topic of people in *Process Innovation*, we feel no guilt about ignoring people in our book. The book was serious, well researched, and hype-free to an extent that it might have been called boring. The book also acknowledged the difficulty of reengineering, pointing out, for example, that it can take five years to reengineer a major process and build the accompanying information systems and people skills. Our confession instead deals with a reengineering topic we didn't really understand until late in the game. That is, we emphasized *process* to the exclusion of *practice*. After reading an important article, "Organizational Learning and Communities of Practice," by John Seely Brown and Paul Duguid, in a somewhat obscure academic journal, we realized our mistake—although just how much to focus on practice and how much on process is a difficult and fascinating question.[11]

Every effort to change how work is done needs a dose of both *process*—the design for how work is to be done—and *practice,* an understanding of how individual workers respond to the real world of work and accomplish their assigned tasks. Process work is engineering, created by teams of analysts or consultants who often have only a dim understanding of how the work they're re-designing is done today. We emphasized that in reengineering, people should be involved in the design of processes, but in writing about reengineering, we and others in the field still very strongly focused on design. Practice work is more like anthropology. To truly understand work practice requires detailed observation and a philosophical acceptance that there are usually good reasons for why workers do things in a particular way. A pure focus on process means that a new design for work is unlikely to be implemented successfully; it probably won't be realistic. A pure focus on practice isn't very helpful either—it leads to a great description of today's work activities, but it may not improve them much.

We now believe that to successfully change work, you've got to have a delicate interplay of process and practice. Some processes can be designed by others and implemented successfully—because they're relatively straightforward to begin with or because it's easy to use people or systems to structure and monitor their performance. Other jobs—particularly those involving knowledge, discretion, and outside interventions from groups like customers or business partners—are very difficult for outsiders to design and require a high proportion of practice orientation. While the complexities of this issue would have made it unlikely for a reengineering book describing both process and practice to be a huge best-seller, the world would have been a better place with such a book.

The worst offenders among purveyors of reengineering approaches (not Hammer and Champy, but later writers on the topic) tried to make the design of new processes a real engineering discipline. They focused heavily, for example, on the modeling language used to describe a business process. Some wanted to model the process, and then automatically generate program code from the model to build the information system that would support the process. Others described in excruciating detail the most rational way to design a best-practice project. Unfortunately, some of these ideas seemed to find a home in the U.S. military, which spent a fortune on reengineering and associated systems activities in the 1990s, but never really got any value other than a lot of process flow diagrams that were never really implemented. When the engineering side of reengineering ran amok, seldom was anything of value achieved in any organization.

Company Implementation Problems

The gurus of reengineering made some mistakes, but then so did the practitioners—at least many of them did. First of all, many managers reinforced the numerous errors made by the gurus. Like us, managers focused too much on process, and not enough on practice—and didn't involve the people who did the work. Like the U.S. military, the managers spent too much time and energy on abstract modeling. Just as some irresponsible writers and consultants generated hyperbole, exaggerated rhetoric, and repackaged ideas in reengineering, so did companies. Corporate communications departments teamed with senior executives to create Advantage 2000, Program 10X, and, perhaps most unfortunately, Project Infinity. They predicted the achievement of radical improvements well before they were achieved. The managers anticipated and trumpeted revolutionary implementation, but got only revolutionary design; the implementation was highly evolutionary (which may have been just as well). As we've noted, in some cases they argued for funding by calling their projects reengineering. The worst offense, of course, was to lay off people and dignify the act as reengineering.

But there were several other, more subtle problems with how companies implemented reengineering that we haven't discussed yet. One is that executives turned too much of their initiatives over to outside firms—both consultants and software vendors. Now, we have worked for several consulting firms, and we wouldn't have accepted our paychecks if we didn't believe that consultants can add value to business change initiatives. But in reengineering, companies commonly let their consultants do almost everything—from interviewing employees about how the current process works, to designing new processes, to providing systems and other capabilities to implement the new processes. None of these activities are objectionable for consultants to perform, but when a company's employees begin to think about a reengineering project as imposed upon them by consultants, there is probably too much influence. We certainly remember many firms that referred to their reengineering initiatives as "the Index project" or "the McKinsey reengineering program." It is, of course, difficult for consultants to turn down work when the client requests it, but senior executives in a company should maintain control of the project and involve employees in doing the work as much as possible. Despite attempts by some consultants to persuade clients that reengineering couldn't be done by mere mortals, there was no real rocket science to the job. And consultants, of course, are as mortal as anyone else!

The other organizations to which reengineering got turned over came along in the latter half of reengineering's golden days— most commonly from 1994 on. Before this, reengineering had encountered a problem. Every new process design required new information systems to provide information to the new process; indeed, one of the core objectives of reengineering was to apply the power of IT to how work gets done. But when it came time to implement all those new information systems, many companies became overwhelmed by the difficulty and cost of building a lot of new systems at once. To their rescue came the vendors of enterprise resource planning systems, or enterprise systems (ES). These systems were, in a sense, the reengineer's dream; they had many positive attributes from the standpoint of reengineered business processes, including the following:

- They worked—that is, they were reliable, secure systems that churned out information the way they were supposed to.

- They were cross-functional, as the newly reengineered business processes were supposed to be.

- They were based on best-practice process designs.

- They supplied a relatively easy way (compared to companies building applications themselves) to automate a broad range of business processes in an integrated fashion.

Not surprisingly, the managers of processes and reengineering projects flocked to the ES vendors SAP, Oracle, PeopleSoft, and so on. Those who were most aware of the reengineering potential of ESs, such as executives at Owens Corning, wrapped up their reengineering and ES implementation projects into one integrated change program. Called Advantage 2000 at Owens Corning, the project involved new processes, new systems, new skills, and predictions of significantly better financial performance. The latter benefit didn't arrive, but there were some extenuating factors (low demand and asbestos lawsuits) that accounted for some of Owens Corning's problems.

But Owens Corning and the many other firms that implemented ESs probably relied too heavily on them as the way to implement reengineering. While the packages were built around best-practice process designs, they were generic rather than specific to a particular company's process designs and business needs. Because it was difficult to modify these systems, most firms ended up with the same processes and information support as every other firm in their industry. Reengineered processes were supposed to yield competitive advantage, but this was impossible with heavy support from an ES. The most competitively oriented companies used an ES for "commodity" processes, but produced their own systems for processes that were critical to competitive advantage. Intel, for example, adopted both reengineering and ES, but did not apply them to the product development and manufacturing processes it deemed core to competitive advantage.

Additionally, many corporate reengineers took on too much change at once. Encouraged by the rhetoric of some gurus, they tried to change multiple processes, big information systems, aspects of organizational structure, and sometimes even business strategy all at once. Such all-encompassing change in a short time frame is difficult, if not impossible. One observer noted that companies that were reengineering multiple processes at once were akin to pilots attempting to change all the engines in a jet airplane at once while flying through the sky. It may be possible, but the risk of failure is great.

Managers also tended to abandon previous approaches to change that had worked well—if somewhat less dramatically—in the past. When reengineering came along, many organizations responded by dropping the management of quality. We've mentioned Nitin Nohria's study of the implementation of quality. In the mid-1990s, he interviewed managers to learn how quality management ideas were introduced and disseminated within companies. Several managers asked, "Why are you asking about quality? We've moved well beyond that to reengineering." Again, however, they may have been led to do so by the unfortunate tendency of some gurus to disparage all foregoing business ideas. Hammer and Champy illustrate this tendency: "None of the management fads of the last twenty years—not management by objectives, diversification, Theory Z, zero-based budgeting, value chain analysis, decentralization, quality circles, 'excellence,' re-structuring, portfolio management, management by walking around, matrix management, intrapreneuring, or one-minute managing—has reversed the deterioration of America's corporate competitive performance. They have only distracted managers from the real task at hand."[12]

The "real task at hand," of course, was reengineering. Our view is that each of these business ideas had something to offer the reflective manager, and we have little doubt that each was of some benefit to some organizations.

The other critical shortcoming of those who implemented reengineering was to treat it as a project rather than a way of life. Processes lose their edge or their fit with organizational and customer requirements over time. The most sophisticated organizations realize that they can never stop improving their business processes—sometimes incrementally, and sometimes radically if the need is there. Reengineering was a short-lived movement during the 1990s. It should have become a permanent addition to the managerial tool kit, to be brought out and applied when process performance falls seriously behind that of competitors or customer expectations.

Are There Good Ideas to Take Away from Reengineering?

Despite the problems with the reengineering movement, you might ask, does it have any ideas worth keeping? You bet. In fact, almost all the ideas within reengineering have substantial merit when used in moderation. Certainly, firms should sometimes address broad, cross-functional processes. And from time to time, they need a serious kick in the pants. Sometimes, as Hammer has noted in a refreshingly serious article about the ongoing role of Six Sigma quality approaches, it is better to throw a broken process away altogether and start from scratch than to improve it incrementally.[13] And IT can no doubt be a powerful enabler and reshaper of processes.

The key is to also remember that reengineering involves risk. Any time an organization needs radical change to deliver the results it needs, it's more likely to fail or to come up short. Like baseball players who swing for the fences or soccer stars who take kicks from midfield, they will miss their goal most of the time. But sometimes desperate moves are called for.

Is Reengineering Coming Back?

When reengineering first appeared in articles and books, the U.S. economy was in recession. In the early years of the twenty-first century, times are tough again, and reengineering is offering itself for another run. Hammer's 2001 book, *The Agenda,* is mostly a restatement of some of the key ideas behind reengineering—customer focus, process management, radical change—albeit with a more subdued tone this time.[14] Companies are clearly interested in cutting costs. Is reengineering the answer to today's economy? Can reengineering overcome its own real problems and its dubious reputation to truly provide value to organizations? And how will it deal with IT this time around?

One attribute of the new reengineering is that it may not be called reengineering. Abandoning that term, with all its baggage, may be the easiest way to signal a new intent. What should the new title be? Champy has obviously been wrestling with this issue. His latest book originally used the term *E-engineering,* but the name was later changed to *X-engineering,* signifying a cross-organizational focus.[15] We could suggest *process innovation,* but that might sound self-serving. Maybe it will be called *Six Sigma* (or one step beyond—*Seven Sigma*), or even something as simple as *process redesign.*

Whatever the name, the next version of reengineering should still be focused on processes, but shouldn't be restricted to the back-office, operational processes that were the primary focus for reengineering in the past. A lot of the value and innovation in organizations today comes from knowledge workers and knowledge work processes, which went largely untouched in the last round of reengineering. These processes—marketing, new product development, strategic planning, and even management—ought to go under the microscope this time.

Of course, knowledge workers and managers will quickly realize that it's not much fun to have their work redesigned by someone else. They will clamor to have a say in how their work gets done. This is reasonable, not only for knowledge workers but for all types of workers. In this go at reengineering, the people who do the work will be much more likely to adopt new processes if they have a hand in designing them.

Much of the buzz about reengineering's return is around the redesign of interorganizational processes. A chapter of Hammer's new book, for example, is devoted to this topic, and all of Champy's is. We would agree that the long-term trend is to create stronger and more automated linkages between suppliers and customers. But companies have been burned before on the difficulty of building such linkages. Remember all the talk in the business-to-business exchange world about how companies in entire industries would integrate their processes and systems so that customers could shop and do deals with any exchange participant? It didn't happen, and now many exchanges are history. The integration proved to be more expensive and time-consuming than most people realized. Some exchanges and industry groups drafted process and information standards for their member companies (RosettaNet comes to mind, and they have done a great job of it), but the firms dragged their feet in implementing the standards. Not only was implementation costly and slow, but succeeding at the standards would lead to the commoditization of their products and competition based only on price. As we learned with internal reengineering, it's much easier to design new processes than to implement them.

In the latter days of reengineering's last visit, enterprise systems emerged as the single technology that could support new cross-functional processes. In fact, reengineering initiatives really turned into ES implementation projects in many companies. The new technologies for this round are more diverse. ESs are still with us and are still the primary backbone for transaction-oriented processes. But ESs are also new. What constitutes an ES is always in flux—today it can address customer service and sales, product development, and analytical processes that weren't even thought of in the early 1990s. The other new tools will vary by the process you are seeking to transform, but include Web services, marketing automation, and collaborative product commerce applications.

With the proliferation of new tools, their integration will continue to be difficult. The goal of cross-functional, cross-business-unit, and cross-organizational integration will continue to be elusive and will undoubtedly inspire a large number of consulting projects.

Since we now know that the big, onetime swing at process change is less likely to succeed than a continuous process-improvement approach, we hope that the new reengineering will combine the incremental, continuous approaches of total quality management or Six Sigma with the power of IT.

Lessons to Remember from Reengineering

Perhaps the most valuable legacy of reengineering is what it has taught us about organizational change and new business ideas. Some of the lessons it provided are the following:

- The inventors of reengineering were middle managers and employees of real companies, not consultants or academics. These are also the people who brought reengineering into companies and made it a reality after the concept became popular. The gurus and CEOs have an important role to play, but they already get too much credit.

- Don't forget that any change must be implemented by people. If people and their desires and behaviors aren't front and center in any new business approach, the approach will probably have a tough time succeeding.

- Don't seize upon the most radical, hype-laden description of the new business idea as the one you want to introduce to your organization. Sure, it can help to get your colleagues in the executive suite excited about a new initiative, but the expectations about what you can accomplish may be raised higher than what you can achieve.

- When a new idea comes along, don't forget about the old ideas. Reengineering should augment rather than replace ideas in many gurus' and managers' minds. No single business idea is all-encompassing or all-powerful.

- Radical change is inherently riskier than incremental change. There's no way around this fact of life. Still, sometimes the risk of radical change is preferable to alternative fates—like going out of business!

- When undertaking a new business idea, managers are all too easily distracted by minor manifestations of the notion—such as ES and process modeling in the case of reengineering. Keep your eyes on the prize.

- Change within a company, where the people involved actually work for you, is likely to be easier than change involving other companies and people not in your employ.

- Revolutionary and violent rhetoric is a bad sign in writing and speaking about a new business idea. Ask yourself why the authors have to work so hard to get your attention.

8

KNOWLEDGE MANAGEMENT

A CASE STORY OF A "P CYCLE" MOVEMENT

THE LIFE CYCLE of the idea of knowledge management (KM) has been very different from that of reengineering. Being more broad-based, KM rose more slowly, wasn't perverted to the same degree as reengineering, and has already persisted longer in organizational and individual agendas than reengineering has. Though KM is not a perfect example of a successful P cycle of a business idea, it comes close. It's still too early to tell whether KM will become pervasive within organizations, but it seems to be heading in that direction.

Serendipitous Progenitors

One fine spring day in 1992, we met over an elegant tea service at the Boston Athenaeum—a historic private library founded in 1807 and used over the years by Nathaniel Hawthorne, Ralph Waldo Emerson, and Louisa May Alcott. We were founders of a sort ourselves—at Ernst & Young we developed a research and "thought leadership" facility. Tom was director of research, and Larry was

179

a program manager. Our organization, the Center for Business Innovation, was located in a charming brownstone building on Boston's Beacon Hill just a few blocks away from the lovely Athenaeum. We liked to go there occasionally (ideally every Wednesday—tea day—but travel and clients usually intervened) to escape our busy office, look out over the patriots' graves in the adjoining Granary Burial Ground, and discuss research strategy, design issues, or personnel problems in the hallowed company of revolutionary ghosts.

On this particular day, we took refuge in the Athenaeum to discuss a multicompany research program called Mastering the Information Environment. Our team designed the program to research how information itself, when managed as an asset, could boost an organization's competitive advantage.[1] Our goal was to focus on information per se, rather than on information technology. IT had already fostered a vast research and managerial literature, but information itself was a field wide open for fresh insights.

Over tea, we haggled over a seemingly flawed premise of the program: information is just a unit of content that helps us understand how people in organizations communicate with one another, learn new practices, and pass on what they learn, but much of it doesn't seem to be valuable and worth managing. As our conversation heated up (cognitively, that that is—we were only drinking tea), we were struggling to articulate a growing conviction that something else—something "not exactly information"—should be our real focus. Information seemed too prosaic and familiar. While munching a tasty lemon square, Tom argued, "We should really be focusing on higher value-added forms of information." Finally Larry looked up and asked, "Don't we really mean knowledge?"

This epiphany on Beacon Hill—while no doubt falling short of previous inspirations at the Athenaeum—led us to reorient our research agenda toward a program that placed knowledge firmly in the center. Knowledge stood in contrast not only to information, but to IT and, of course, data. Thus we launched what we believe was the first multicompany research program devoted to knowledge management. For us, this decision and this program were instrumental in developing insights on this relatively new topic. It brought us into contact with various firms' idea practitioners who were already beginning to manage what their organizations knew.

Intellectual Progenitors

Before proceeding with our knowledge-centered program, we had to step back and look at our intellectual antecedents. The study of knowledge—or epistemology—lies beyond the scope of this book, and we'll leave such study in the able hands of philosophers and classicists. But it is often useful to know from what perspective an idea comes, and the idea of knowledge has developed beyond philosophy across the disciplines—starting with economics, then turning to sociology and information management. The multiple directions from which knowledge derives have helped to nourish its progression from the genteel library stacks to its presence in meeting rooms, bookstores, and conference halls across the world.

Potential users of knowledge management as an idea for businesses could take comfort from the economic roots of the subject. In *The Wealth of Nations,* the economist Adam Smith noted that repetition of a task continuously shortened the time needed to achieve the desired results—an observation that gestures toward understanding knowledge as a resource. The great Victorian economist Alfred Marshall took it a step further, discussing knowledge as a valuable form of productive force.

However, economic analyses of knowledge did not take an analytical turn until World War II, when urgent incentives to improve aircraft production time impelled the armed forces to employ newly developed tools of statistical analysis. The analyses suggested that workers really did learn from their own experience, and it could finally be proven. In the 1950s the newly formed RAND Corporation think tank further developed these ideas, which were later expressed by Nobel Prize winner Kenneth Arrow in his classic article on learning by doing.[2]

After Arrow, knowledge economics split into three overlapping branches, some of which have yielded Nobel Prizes. The first branch, the study of human capital, mainly developed by Theodore Schultz and Gary Becker, gauges the economic value of an individual's knowledge as measured by his or her education, training, and work experience. Development economists and theorists such as Paul Romer and Richard Nelson follow a second branch of inquiry by studying the role of knowledge and knowledge outputs in building national capabilities and institutions. Economists of the third branch (including Sid Winter, David Teece, Giovanni Dosi, and Keith Pavitt) investigate how knowledge both enables organizational innovations and constitutes the core of organizational routines and processes.

Sociology is another discipline that helped develop managerial knowledge concepts. The roots of the *sociology of knowledge* go back to the nineteenth century, and sociologists established early on that knowledge creation and use are social processes. Instead of focusing on only the economic value of knowledge, many sociologists demonstrated how the shift to a knowledge-based economy affects organizations, countries, and regions. Certainly, Harvard sociologist Daniel Bell's *Coming of Post-Industrial Society* inspired many of us to think about how the functions of knowledge will change in the economy of the 1980s onward.[3] Sociologists also spoke of social networks and "invisible colleges" of knowledge producers and users, presaging the idea of the community of practice. Journalists with a sociological bent, like Alvin Toffler, also helped popularize sociological ideas about knowledge. Toffler's popular book, *Future Shock*, translated the sociology of knowledge into a managerial frame of reference.[4]

A third discipline, once loosely called information management, also made significant intellectual contributions to KM.

Economist Fritz Machlup's anthology, *Information,* is an exemplary artifact of the movement in its early stages.[5] Machlup took an integrated approach to how information (and often knowledge) "works" and is enacted within organizations. As such, information management attracted practitioners from across the disciplines: Economists, sociologists, cognitive scientists, library scientists, computer scientists, psychologists, and polymaths like Herbert Simon were all drawn to the movement. But information management never quite made it as a separate discipline, and many of its theorists retreated back to their original fields. The movement's main contribution was to redirect the focus of many thinkers (ourselves included) to information, rather than technology, as a source of value.

Some major contributions to the growth of KM do not fit neatly into any category. Scientist Michael Polanyi, for example, was Einstein's research assistant before he developed an interest in policy and philosophy. Polanyi carried out his fundamental insight, "We know more than we can say," in his well-known two books, *The Tacit Dimension* and *Personal Knowledge.*[6] MIT professor Donald Schoen was inspired by Polanyi to write *The Reflective Practitioner,* which claims that knowledge is mostly tacit and reveals itself in actions and decisions made by practitioners.[7]

Riding the Wave

When we began to work on fleshing out the nascent idea of knowledge management, we were not alone in our endeavor, and our program helped us interact with both leading practitioners and other researchers launching KM projects. Nevertheless, some of our fellow researchers and consultants dismissed the subject as too ephemeral and vague. Consultants oriented to large-scale systems integration assignments were not always comfortable leaving the safety zone of technology and data to try to sell the nebulous new idea of knowledge. Reactions ranging from active resistance to apathy were no surprise to us. New ideas challenge people to read, think, test, develop, and persuade others—they require time and energy.

Conservative organizations and managers generally follow current practice instead of initiating new ideas themselves. The successful, but hardly innovative, head of sales for the consulting firm we worked for at the time told us, "No client has asked me for services around this. Why should we support it further?" His position was pragmatic—that the firm should only invest in services after clients had expressed a strong interest. We asked, what would we have to sell our clients once they expressed an interest? His solution was that in the unlikely event someone did so, we could "cobble something together," using published news stories, quick interviews, hastily improvised methods, and the like. His approach wasn't necessarily wrong, but it was fortunate that he wasn't in charge of research or innovation.

However, we had a secret weapon—a far-flung network of idea practitioners with a bent toward knowledge. Already pursuing their own KM ideas and projects, they were eager to join our program. Interestingly, our network did not overlap with the networks of our consulting partners. When we showed the list of our knowledge clients to a senior consultant at Ernst & Young who knew people in almost every member firm, he knew none of our members. Most consultants were selling established ideas to established managers, whereas we were selling to a breed apart.

Zeitgeist

KM turned out to be a zeitgeist idea, an idea in sync with the spirit of the times. Imagine that all management ideas are available all the time, but that they will only catch on when they flow in alignment with currents in society and the economy. The zeitgeist factor cautions idea practitioners not only to choose their battles wisely, but also to choose their timing wisely. KM was a well-timed battle.

How did the timing work for KM? Perhaps the most important coincident factor was the rise of knowledge-oriented technologies. Previous information technologies were much better suited to managing data in structured formats. Then Lotus introduced its Notes product, Tim Berners-Lee invented the World Wide Web, and many smaller vendors introduced collaboration tools. Each of these technologies was able to handle textual and graphic forms of information and knowledge. If not for their availability, KM would never have taken off.

The KM movement also fell into sync with the fervor around economic globalization. As companies spread their people and products around the world, they needed a means to spread knowledge globally as well. Not much was written in the popular press about the relationship between the two, but globalization and KM both picked up steam in the early 1990s. The consequences of globalization compelled executive interest in KM. There are, of course, still challenges in sharing far-flung knowledge, but a comprehensive KM program can certainly help.

Globalization also facilitated the growth of knowledge-based businesses. As commodity manufacturing and service businesses moved to the lowest-cost part of the world in which they could be produced, firms in more expensive and sophisticated economies had to move upscale. Firms that still try to manufacture or provide technology-based services in advanced economies find they can no longer turn a profit. These firms must turn toward knowledge-based services, or products with knowledge embedded in the product.

Legitimization: Publishing

One of the crucial junctures of any idea movement is when and how it becomes legitimized—a process that is part overt, part tacit. As discussed in chapter 5, an idea is legitimized when it's perceived as developed, evaluated, and used to good effect by people and organizations with sound credentials.

We believe we offered in 1994 the first public conference on knowledge management. When we tried to drum up speakers and attendees, we heard, "What is KM?" and "What are you guys talking about?" We held the modestly successful affair in Boston with about eighty curiosity seekers and perhaps thirty KM practitioners and commentators. A mere six years later in 2000, there were more than fifty KM conferences offered throughout the world in one year alone. The movement had become legitimized.

What had happened in the intervening years? The idea of KM had gained credentials. One of the earliest written salvos came from Tom Peters's *Liberation Management,* a huge business hit of 1991. Coauthor of *In Search of Excellence,* one of the best-selling business books ever, Peters had credentials.[8] He gave lectures everywhere, his face was omnipresent in business magazines, and his books were prominently displayed. *Liberation Management* introduced the world to a group of people at McKinsey & Company, especially Brook Manville, who was attempting to create a KM capability. The book presented the practice's adventures with KM as a mix of the Manhattan Project and a rock concert. The publicity made Manville the best-known KM idea practitioner. His lectures and interviews further broadened the exposure of the new concept.

Another important stroke of credentials came from journalist Tom Stewart. In a 1991 cover story, Stewart introduced *Fortune* magazine readers not only to KM, but to intellectual capital, invisible assets, and the other rhetorical flourishes that enliven the concept.[9] Stewart gained credentials for the movement in three ways: He alerted the business world to what early KM practitioners were doing, he published his pieces in respected business magazines that confer their own credibility, and he wrote two well-received books that enhanced the reputation of several KM practitioners and theorists. Like Manville, these newly popular practitioners were empowered by the books to carry the movement forward.

A third form of credentialism came from academia. At our first knowledge conference, we managed to convince Harvard

Business School professor Chris Bartlett to speak for us. Bartlett is a strategy scholar well known for his articles on multinational and multidivisional management. He was reluctant to speak about knowledge at first, but he ended up giving an excellent speech on the role of knowledge in strategizing and running large, complex organizations, and became the first academic to speak on the topic of knowledge in this context.

At about the same time, Japanese professors Ikujiro Nonaka and Hirotaka Takeuchi studied the use of knowledge in Asian firms in Nonaka's acclaimed *Harvard Business Review* article and their book by the same name, *The Knowledge-Creating Company*.[10] Theirs is still the best available source on tacit knowledge and knowledge creation, particularly in Japan. Shortly thereafter, a Harvard Business School professor, Dorothy Leonard, wrote on similar topics from a U.S. perspective and added to the movement's credentials with her lectures and her 1995 book, *Wellsprings of Knowledge*.[11] One case study within the book—on Chaparral Steel—was the first study of how a whole company reinvented itself around knowledge. The next major contribution was our own *Working Knowledge*, an outgrowth of our multiclient research program on KM that documented knowledge management practices in over fifty firms and outlines the management lessons they prove.[12] By the end of the 1990s, articles on KM had appeared in *Harvard Business Review, Sloan Management Review,* and every other prestigious management journal.

As an aside to credentialing the topic through publishing, eventually universities even got around to adding credentials to KM by teaching the subject. We believe that our course at the University of Texas business school in 1995 was the first on KM. Today, many business schools have courses in KM, and there are even several degree programs on the subject.

Other institutions also helped to legitimize the topic of KM through publishing and conferences. The American Productivity and Quality Center (APQC), led by Carla O'Dell, established a program of multicompany research projects, annual conferences, and articles and book publishing that was quite successful. By

2002, the APQC had conducted ten separate studies on KM and had greatly advanced the KM topic of best practices. The Conference Board, whose efforts in KM were led by Brian Hackett (also a fan of new business ideas in general), also conducted studies on KM and put on an annual knowledge and learning conference, at least through 2002.

The collected weight of these publications, academic reputations, and organizational support added a huge amount of credibility to KM. What was in the early 1990s a somewhat crackpot idea became accepted management practice by the end of the decade. Pioneering idea practitioners had to be truly brave to adopt the idea at the beginning, but it became an easy decision to champion KM a few years later.

Legitimization Through Stories of Pilots and Programs

Grassroots legitimization comes through documented practice and examples of the success of actual KM initiatives. These stories are disseminated not only through publications, but also in conferences. Presentations of KM practitioners are an important feature of every KM conference. These talks allow would-be practitioners to "kick the tires" of an idea—to listen to and question those who claim to have had success with KM. The audience's trust of the presenter is a vital, yet rarely researched, phenomenon. As Woody Allen said, "Sincerity is a great thing—if you can fake it, you've got it made."

We have personal experience of the power of the presenter from our work with British Petroleum (BP). In the early 1990s, the firm's new managing director, John Browne, developed an early interest in knowledge practices. He asked his CIO, John Cross, to undertake some modest but well-thought-out projects involving tacit knowledge development and transfer across the firm's many drilling and operational sites. Cross asked several teams to do knowledge-oriented investigations and then funded the teams to go forth and explain their findings. BP's then director of organizational development, Kate Owen, told us that the firm prefers to hire highly articulate people as managers, a policy that pays off at conferences. BP's KM project managers included Kent Greenes (now chief knowledge officer at systems integrator SAIC), Keith Pearce, and Chris Collinson, all of whom made presentations at more than a hundred conferences and meetings (as estimated by Greenes) between 1993 and 2000. They spoke in detail of the company's success with knowledge initiatives. They always got the audience's attention by enumerating the hefty sums, often hundreds of thousands or millions of pounds, saved or made through the knowledge projects.[13]

BP presenters deviated from the analytic, "Isn't KM wonderful?" presentation of their projects, and instead developed compelling practice stories. Whether we call them cases, narratives, histories, benchmarking examples, or exemplars, they follow a remarkably similar pattern. It goes something like this: An organization is in a stable state when a knowledge intervention occurs. The organization changes what it knows, how it knows, or how it shares what it knows. This causes the organization to enter a new phase with added, distributed, or enhanced knowledge. Consequently, the organization enjoys greater profitability or productivity. These sorts of stories, the mother's milk of any management movement, proliferated as the KM movement spread.

Sometimes, among a group of related stories, a line emerges that seems to capture the theme of the movement. When Gertrude Stein quipped, "They are all a lost generation," she pulled together a scraggly group of American expatriates and made them a movement. John Doyle, the former head of Hewlett-Packard Labs, is credited with a similar galvanizing remark, "If only HP knew what HP knows." This phrase is still a powerful presence as KM makes its global progress. It summarizes an important KM principle in a pithy manner and has actually caught on globally. We've heard it used at a variety of companies; just substitute your own company's name for HP's.

No discussion of practice and stories would be complete without mention of Steve Denning and his success at The World Bank. Many KM practitioners have expressed envy of Denning. The bank strives to hire only "the best and the brightest." It has plenty of knowledge-focused technologies in place, and most important, it has had the strong support of its outspoken president, James Wolfensohn, who publicly proclaimed that The World Bank should henceforth be known as The Knowledge Bank! What could be a more fertile climate for the flourishing of an idea?

However, as Denning has eloquently documented in his auto-biographical study of storytelling at the bank, much did go wrong until he decided to use stories to demonstrate how KM practices were adding very substantially to the bank's work throughout the world.[14] Previously, Denning had used the same dullish analytics that we all use (or used to use) in describing our projects. This involved PowerPoint presentations with pie or bar charts showing cost reductions or some quantitative return on the project in question. But the idea practitioner found that he was not getting traction or much support for his knowledge staff from the use of these tired techniques. When he converted to stories (he has always loved literature), Denning made much more progress. Skeptics were more likely to be converted by a well-formed anecdote than by statistics. Denning, like others mentioned here, also began to appear at conferences and association presentations discussing KM at The World Bank and how stories contributed to their success. His stories about stories have become legendary in KM circles.

Perspective to Pervasiveness

So what was accomplished in KM in a decade or so? In 1992, when we first began to offer KM as a subject for conference presentations, there were few takers. Today, no executive committee, board, or other management forum would likely reject a

Steve Denning, Idea Practitioner

Australian born and raised, Steve Denning has been one of the more enduring idea practitioners within the KM movement. Denning first studied law and psychology at Sydney University and then moved to Oxford University, where he took a further degree in legal studies. While at Oxford, he saw a recruiting notice for The World Bank, and intrigued by both the bank's mission and the prospect of more world travel, he signed on and stayed for more than thirty years.

Denning's career, like that of many other idea practitioners, has encompassed several movements. For example, he has been a member of the bank's Quality Council as well as director of various African development departments. In 1996 he was appointed one of the first program directors for KM anywhere.

Denning's approach to "selling" KM at The World Bank had much to do with his innovative approach to telling stories—stories about how knowledge projects actually worked and succeeded within bank projects. His experiences in using stories this way were documented in his lively and enlightening book, *The Springboard*.

Although he has left the bank as an employee, Denning still consults there. He spends his time reading voraciously, writing poems and novels, and speaking and consulting on knowledge-based issues and how stories encapsulate and communicate knowledge: a Renaissance man, indeed!

substantive or innovative knowledge proposal. The subject, however defined, has achieved a permanent place at the management table, and most large commercial organizations have projects under way. The Organisation for Economic Cooperation and Development (OECD) is currently running a census of KM projects among its members. Early results indicate that the number of KM projects, even in modest-sized firms, is increasing and runs well into the thousands. We have seen KM projects in the United States, the United Kingdom, Scandinavia, Australia, Singapore, Korea, Germany, Italy, the Netherlands, South Africa, and Brazil. For all we know, there's one under way in Antarctica. In addition to all the corporate initiatives, many government agencies and departments have taken up KM projects, which are also on the rise in nongovernmental organizations such as The World Bank, International Monetary Fund, and the United Nations.

On the academic front, at least three research institutes are dedicated to better understanding knowledge, and courses on KM are now taught at more than thirty business schools worldwide. At least three Ph.D. programs in KM are offered by academic institutions. Several academic journals, including *Organization Science, Strategic Management Review,* and the *Journal of Management Information Systems,* have published special issues on KM in the late 1990s and thereafter. Numerous business researchers in the strategy and organizational behavior fields are working on how to incorporate knowledge into their models and structures. Even some industrial economists are struggling to build theories that allow for the central role of knowledge in firm and overall economic performance.

Personal experience illustrates how KM has entered the common parlance. Since 1995, we have had the word *knowledge* somewhere on our business cards. A few years ago, we would expect that a recipient of the card—say, a fellow airline passenger— would be befuddled. More recently, people generally recognize the term *knowledge management,* and many are curious enough to strike up a conversation about it.

The language of KM is everywhere in evidence. *Communities of practice,* a term invented and popularized by KM researchers, is ubiquitous in discussion and print. *Intellectual capital* is a term so common, it is used in popular advertisements. The very word *knowledge* springs up in product literature and ads for natural foods. Knowledge work and knowledge workers are the subjects of conferences, books, analyst reports, and U.S. government–issued reports. Countless OECD, Work Bank, and European Union reports have the word *knowledge* in their titles.

Knowledge management has been successful in part because it avoided some of the excesses of other new management ideas, such as reengineering. As KM acquired the trappings of academic and business respectability, its gurus and practitioners generally avoided extravagant claims for what could be accomplished through the concept. Unlike reengineering, KM wasn't associated with claims of tenfold improvement in corporate performance or with radical reductions in head count. Fortunately, no one invented a means of extracting knowledge from people's heads that was so effective that the people would no longer be needed in companies. As a result, expectations never got too high for KM, and they were not dashed on the rocks of reality.

Knowledge management did have problems as a new business idea, however. One issue was that too many people—particularly IT vendors—conflated the use of knowledge technologies with the successful management of knowledge. Sometimes this was done in rather obvious ways. One of us, for example, remembers speaking at a KM conference in Florida. At the beginning of the conference, each attendee's seat was graced with a new publication, *KM World*. How nice, we thought—KM now has its own little newspaper. On examination, however, we discovered that the paper was chock-full of press releases from imaging and document management technology vendors, with only a thin veneer of KM articles on the front page. Only the previous week it had been known as *Imaging World*. Despite the tendency of vendors to seize upon KM as the answer to their marketing prayers, most users of the KM idea seemed to realize that social, cultural, and organizational factors were more important to their success than technology, and that they couldn't be bought from a vendor. The technology focus never became overwhelming.

Another problem was that KM became all things to all people. The idea started out with a strong focus on using technology to manage textual knowledge on "best practices" and "lessons learned." But knowledge is a broad and important subject, and over time KM evolved to include such topics as organizational learning, technology transfer, competitive intelligence, data warehousing and business intelligence, document management, and many other related ideas. With so much bundled into the idea, KM couldn't help but disappoint. This is no doubt a key reason why executives rated KM low in terms of user satisfaction in Bain & Company's "Management Tools and Techniques" Survey in 2001.

On the positive side, however, the diversity of knowledge management may have contributed to its longevity. Whereas reengineering rose and fell within five years, we've observed a high degree of interest in KM over a decade now, and it doesn't seem to be waning. Some "bibliometric" research bears this out. Len Ponzi and Mike Koenig of Long Island University suggest that many management fads peak in terms of articles and books in five years or so.[15] Knowledge management publications, however, did not decline after five years, but rather continued to grow and prosper—at least on paper. The researchers suggest that this growth may indicate that KM is becoming an accepted aspect of business and management. That's exactly our hypothesis as well. Warts and all, KM, we believe, is well on its way to pervasiveness. If you fancy yourself an idea practitioner and have managed to ignore KM thus far, it's time to stop waiting.

9

IDEA-BASED LEADERSHIP

HOW CAN YOUR ORGANIZATION LEAD WITH IDEAS?

ONE ASPECT that we have largely ignored in discussing idea-based change in organizations is the role of leaders. Of course, books about leaders and leadership abound, and we didn't want to write yet another. To be honest, at one point we considered referring to the primary subject of this book—the people who work with ideas for a living—as idea leaders, rather than idea practitioners. These individuals certainly need to exhibit some attributes of leadership if they're going to be successful; we've attempted to describe some of these attributes throughout this book.

But there is also little doubt that leaders other than idea practitioners are necessary for the successful execution of business and management ideas. An idea practitioner without the support and protection of an idea-oriented leader is unlikely to get very far. In this chapter, therefore, we describe what idea-based leadership is all about. If you are a leader of your organization, you can learn how to facilitate idea-based change and how to make the jobs of idea practitioners easier and more successful. If you're not a senior leader within your company or organization, reading this chapter may help you elicit the idea-friendly behaviors from your leaders that you need. We'll quote a number of our idea practitioners in this chapter on their relationships with leaders, but since that's a somewhat touchy subject, we'll keep the quotes anonymous.

There's one other group in addition to leaders and idea practitioners whom we haven't mentioned: the people who do the work. Sometimes called the grass roots by idea practitioners, these are the people whose behavior has to change if any idea is going to be successful in your organization. Leaders, idea practitioners, and the grass roots must be involved in any idea-centered change process, as we heard in one interview: "Leadership sets the vision, the rhetoric, but grass roots supply the will. These are the current and the circuitry of building ideas. The single-sided 'monarch' approach—which includes tremendous funding—will always fail or damage the idea if there isn't grassroots buy-in." Although it's difficult to generalize about everyone who's not a leader or an idea practitioner, we'll describe their key roles at various points in this chapter.

We began this book with a contrast between the idea orientations of General Electric and Westinghouse. We'll return to GE in this chapter, simply because it's the best in the world at idea-driven business transformation. We discuss several of GE's approaches throughout this chapter, which we conclude with excerpts from our interview of one of GE's (and by extension, the world's) most successful idea practitioners, Steve Kerr. Kerr discusses not only his idea practitioner role, but also the relationship between his work and the leadership of Jack Welch. The words of one of the world's most successful idea practitioners at one of the world's most successful companies should be inspiring to anyone even remotely interested in business ideas.

What Do Leaders Do with Ideas?

Why should leaders embrace new business and management ideas? As we've argued throughout this book, ideas are critical to enhanced business performance, to the motivation of workers, and to organizational vitality. As one of our idea practitioners put it: "Leaders have to be committed to cultural renewal, particularly in older firms. Idea practitioners can help them do that."

Leaders of organizations don't have to be idea practitioners themselves. On top of all the other things leaders have to do, it's understood that they may not have the time or energy to scan for ideas, modify them to suit their own organizations, and implement them successfully. But they do have key responsibilities in idea-based change, which will describe in the following sections.

Ensure the Presence and Respect of Idea Practitioners

Idea practitioners are an incredibly valuable resource for organizations, but they don't pop up and flourish at random. They have to be recruited, their careers nourished, and their successes rewarded. That said, the role can be an informal one. We don't necessarily think it's a good idea to establish an "idea management" function—better to have idea-related activities embedded throughout the rest of the business. And having idea practitioners around isn't hugely expensive, either. Most idea practitioners have other jobs, and play their idea roles somewhat on the margin. However, there should be some clarity and recognition with respect to who is playing the role within an organization. A company's leadership team ought to know on whom they can rely to bring in new ideas and nurture them. These might be scattered around the organization—an operationally oriented idea person in manufacturing, one who's particularly oriented to customer ideas and innovation in marketing, and a strategic ideas specialist in, of course, strategic planning.

They have to be the right people, too. Let's be frank: some pretenders to the idea practitioner role can be a bit flaky. There are many ways they can go off-track. They become "true believers" in an idiosyncratic notion that may have little appeal to others. They may seek out idea practitioner roles because they're incapable of managing their way out of a paper bag. Maybe they're slavish groupies to some charismatic guru. Or they're just out of business school, hoping to keep up contact with a beloved professor.

Leaders have to ensure that their idea practitioners have none of these attributes. They must be mature, wise, productive, and respected individuals. They must be aware of the perils inherent in the statement, "I'm from corporate, and I'm here with a better idea." They must be simultaneously modest and confident. They must be well-read and well-versed in the art and science of management, without being pedantic. They must be passionate about ideas for their own sake and for the sake of business change, but not for the sake of advancing their own careers. Of course, such people are hard to find, and hard to keep.

We're not quite sure what a recruiting strategy for idea practitioners would involve, although it's clear from the backgrounds of our interviewees that a lot of education—often in the liberal arts—is a prerequisite. Several of our idea practitioners were even professors (including Steve Kerr), so you should cultivate relationships at universities. Perhaps the best recruiting strategy is simply to identify those idea practitioners who are already within your organization, but not yet identified as such.

A retention strategy, however, is easier to prescribe. Idea practitioners need reward and recognition. They need freedom to pursue ideas. They need the attention of leaders. They need the resources to make ideas a reality. Even more than most employees, they are not primarily motivated by money or power, but by intellectual stimulation and seeing ideas bloom into action. One practitioner described the power of being given a "mandate" to implement an idea: "We didn't have much of an organizational hierarchy. But I was given a mandate from the CEO—a very rare thing at the company—to pull off this particular idea. If anybody questioned it, I could say, 'Bob wants this to happen.' And that made all the difference."

Set Forth an Idea Strategy and an Idea-Friendly Culture

An organization can't work effectively with ideas if leaders don't set up a strategy and culture that lets the right ideas flourish. General Electric is—at least in recent years—a model for this culture. While Jack Welch was known in his early days as insensitive to human and social issues, in his later years as CEO he became very oriented to establishing a culture that facilitated the creation and flow of ideas. He credits a great deal of GE's success and growth to its "social architecture," which both emerged from the ideas GE pursued and enhanced their success. The architecture has three components:

- **Dialogue:** from anyone in the company to anyone in the company (this principle was discovered and nourished through the Work-Out process described in Chapter 1);

- **Boundarylessness:** Welch refers to this principle as "maximizing individual and collective intellect" from within and outside the company (it was initially advocated by Steve Kerr, an interview with whom comes later in this chapter);

- **Trust and Responsibility:** These principles allow people to learn effectively from each other and provide motivation for putting ideas to work.

These simple cultural components are not unique to GE, but they have been applied and managed with particular effectiveness there.

It's also up to leaders to signal that ideas of a certain type will be welcomed. For example, is this a time within the company for ideas related to either efficiency, effectiveness, or innovation? The top 300 people at one of the companies we studied, for example, were brought together to discuss innovation and the ideas related to that broad theme.

Leaders also need to decide how aggressively the organization will pursue ideas. Will it embrace the idea, or experiment with it? One of the idea practitioners we interviewed called the former approach "jumping on the tiger": "We knew we needed large-scale cultural change; that's what jumping on the tiger is all about. We'd grown nearly 250% in 10 years, but how were we going to continue it? Our CEO knew that only a wholehearted embrace of the right ideas could support that kind of growth."

It's been said often that innovation requires the ability to fail, and innovation driven by business and management ideas is no exception. Some ideas will not work out, despite the best intentions and efforts. According to one idea practitioner at a services firm: "This kind of culture is based in open dialogue, where being wrong is not fatal to your career, but expected. Ideas are tweaked and made vital this way. These cultures exhibit ratios in which one in ten ideas gets through and is implemented . . . "

One might argue, in fact, that the experiments undertaken with business and management ideas are more difficult and complex than those in any laboratory, yet no one expects that all laboratory experiments will succeed.

We should also note that the basic values of an organization play an important role in setting the boundaries for exploring ideas. If values are clearly stated, managers and employees can freely explore ideas that remain within those boundaries. At Johnson & Johnson, for example, the values of the organization are clearly articulated in the firm's famous "Credo." Mike Burtha, a prominent idea practitioner at J&J, feels that the Credo gives him a framework for exploring business ideas. What management approaches would bring the company closer to realizing the values in the Credo? As long as his work reflects and builds on the context of the Credo, he feels comfortable taking risks with ideas. "For me, it provides a relevant foundation for my idea generation process," he says. "As long as I'm staying in that framework of values, I know I'll be okay."

Work with Idea Practitioners on Each Idea

Leaders can't rest once idea practitioners are in place. The successful implementation of each idea is a dynamic interplay between the leader, the idea practitioner, and the grassroots employees. If the leader has a trusting relationship with the idea practitioner, ideas will flow back and forth; leaders can feed ideas they hear about to the idea practitioner for analysis and modification, and idea practitioners can run ideas by leaders to see if they are worthy of support. Idea practitioners can also be a sounding board for leaders as to how particular ideas might fare in the organization. Such a close relationship might have prevented the problem described to us by an idea practitioner in a technology firm: "Our CEO said, 'We're going to improve hardware quality by a factor of ten over ten years.' This was very successful. Then he advocated the same idea in a different place—software, but by a factor of ten over five years. This was a flop. Our management knew that the market didn't want quality in software; timing was more important than quality. He was never able to get management's buy-in, because they knew it wasn't going to help their business."

The leader can work with the idea practitioner to, as one of our interviewees put it, "build a logic between the idea and the firm." The idea can be couched in terms of the firm's specific situation and needs. A marketing campaign can be built. Early adopters can be selected. Leaders can advise idea practitioners on how to get other leaders and managers to "put some skin in the game." One idea practitioner described the process: "I rely on my immediate manager to socialize the concepts I work with, and to prepare his colleagues for upcoming opportunities. Then, there is usually one other senior manager who 'gets it' and is willing to put his or her organization on the line to pilot the ideas, learn about them, and go forward."

Then the idea must be taken to the streets. All the normal principles about change management apply. Our practitioners described it as a combination of top down, bottom up, and middle out: "I try to work both sides toward the middle in terms of ideas, but this means you must participate in a dance. The bottom-up method tends to be 'show and tell.' I like to call it benchmarking, but basically you're finding users who are using or doing whatever it is you want to show, and putting them on the stage."

One idea practitioner whose organization works with franchisees noted that the idea of grass roots goes well beyond employees: "Any idea that's going to reach the end consumer has to deal with a 'three-legged stool.' There are our employees, our owner-operators, and our suppliers. . . . This consensus style of an idea sell-in has been successful for long-term initiatives. It is not, however, a system that works with speed."

The last responsibility of the leader relative to idea practitioners is to ensure that the practitioners end up in a good position after the idea has run its course or has become embedded within the organization. If idea practitioners don't prosper from taking a leading position on ideas, then other people in the organization won't push ideas. GE, for example, tries to ensure that the business unit leaders of idea initiatives such as digitization emerge with good jobs. Gerry Podesta, who led the e-business initiative at GE Plastics, was promoted to head of GE Plastics for the Americas after e-business was embedded within other business functions.

Signal the Importance of Ideas

Leaders signal the importance of ideas with their words, symbolic acts, and their own behaviors—even when they don't realize it. We've already described in chapter 8 a great example of a positive signal: James Wolfensohn's telling the world's finance ministers that The World Bank was going to become The Knowledge Bank. This set in motion a highly successful pursuit of KM ideas.

We've seen many other types of signals—some explicit, and others subtle. If you want real change, explicit is better. For example, when Jack Welch was championing e-business and digitization at GE, he noted that the opportunities and threats created by the Internet were "the biggest change I have seen at GE" and "number one, two, three and four on my agenda." That advocacy, of course, sends a very powerful message. If any e-business leaders missed it, Welch left nothing to chance, assert Chris Bartlett and Meg Glinska: "In typical fashion, he began calling personally on the newly appointed e-business leaders to ensure there was sufficient urgency and boldness in their actions. And at every encounter he would ask them how much they were selling over the Internet, and what more they could be doing. 'It's a great job because Jack is into it,' said one. 'And it's a terrible job because Jack is into it.'"[1]

Other leaders are generally less direct than Welch in their advocacy for ideas and could signal their interest in other ways:

- Send out an organizationwide memo or an organization-wide broadcast.

- At a staff meeting, ask how each member of the executive team is addressing the idea.

- Introduce the idea's key guru at a management meeting, and meet with the guru privately to discuss the idea's implementation at the company.

- Keep a copy of a thoughtful book about the idea on your credenza.

All of these, of course, would be positive signals.

As we noted, sometimes the signaling involves the leader himself or herself, and sometimes it means providing a mandate, or "air cover," for the idea practitioner. One idea practitioner drew on this military analogy: "Leaders need to provide high-level cover—like a strategic air command. Idea practitioners have to figure out an organization's rejection mechanisms. Leaders have to clear a path for you to keep the idea protected, so that it can continue to spread. When you have high-level cover at the executive level, you can make sure that it works and it's going to last—as opposed to being a fad, which can ruin an organization's capacity for ideas for a long time."

Leaders sometimes fail to send the right signal about ideas because of conflicting priorities. Perhaps they like a particular idea and want to see it propagated, but at the same time there are other ideas getting more money and attention. This problem cropped up for one idea practitioner: "The two biggest showstoppers that I've seen are actual budget constraints and conflicting priorities. Often in our organization, everyone is extremely busy, working on several goals/projects simultaneously. There is often little time to reflect on and learn about new ideas. It can be difficult, for example, to implement any new idea during the budget cycle, when management's attention is consumed by next year's budget. When we were trying to implement a balanced scorecard, for example, . . . management needed to devote time to develop an understanding of it, but they were consumed with achieving other goals."

No magic nostrum can solve the problem of insufficient management attention, but leaders need to ensure that the ideas that get attention are those that should be getting attention. If there simply isn't enough attention available for a new idea, perhaps consultants can be called in to help.

On the truly negative side, leaders can quash ideas (deliberately or accidentally) with caustic, paralyzing rhetoric. One idea practitioner described a leader's single-minded and negative attitude: "He always said, 'Don't make us better, make us money.' Even training can't undo the culture that a leader's 'make us money' attitude creates. The other variation was, 'If you're going to show me significant payback, then great.' But these naysayers know that ideas don't always have quick, significant payback."

Leaders can also go too far in the other direction and encourage a culture of faddism. As we've noted, organizations with faddish tendencies embrace too many ideas, seek out the most sensational versions of those ideas, and drop old ideas when new ones come along. Faddish leaders may also cynically adopt ideas on the surface, only to hide their real intent—as when many companies announced that they were "reengineering" and would need to lay off thousands of workers as a result. But the reengineering had nothing to do with the layoffs; the leaders adopted the term, not the idea.

What does an idea practitioner do when the leadership and organization aren't open or friendly to ideas? This is a tough one. We've found in our experiences with students, colleagues, and consulting clients that it's very difficult to stimulate or motivate people with ideas if intellectual curiosity is lacking. Perhaps such curiosity is transmitted genetically, and we either have it or we don't. If leaders have no intellectual curiosity, then it may be time for an idea practitioner to practice his or her ideas elsewhere.

Interview with Steve Kerr

To end this chapter on a cheerier note, we turn to our interview with Steve Kerr, who seems to end up at organizations where ideas matter, and where leaders play important roles in establishing idea-driven change. Kerr is now chief learning officer of Goldman Sachs (see sidebar). He ran General Electric's Crotonville Leadership Institute from 1994 to 2001. As an idea practitioner, he receives extraordinary leadership and organizational support. We believe that Kerr offers a powerful first-person account of how to be an effective idea practitioner at some of the world's top firms.

Steven Kerr, Idea Practitioner

Steve Kerr has a somewhat unusual background—even for an idea practitioner. He's as close to a hybrid practitioner-guru as anyone will find. Before entering GE, he was professor and dean at University of Southern California's Marshall School of Business, and also a professor at Ohio State University and the University of Michigan. He is an expert on leadership development and motivation. Although his most recent roles have centered around the advocacy and implementation of business ideas inside organizations, Kerr has also written dozens of articles and several books, including *The GE Work-Out*, *The Boundaryless Organization*, and *Ultimate Rewards*. His 1975 article, "On the Folly of Rewarding A, While Hoping for B," is one of the most widely cited sources in the management literature on compensation issues. Kerr's point is that people will (quite rationally) do what they are rewarded to do, rather than what their organization says they should do.

We interviewed Kerr on a muggy June day in his (thankfully) air-conditioned thirtieth-floor office at the Goldman Sachs headquarters in downtown Manhattan.

Why did you go to GE?

Let's start with the high-level reasons. As an educator, I presumed the best place and platform to work with ideas was to be found in an academic institution. Every time Welch asked me to come work for GE, I therefore declined. After five weeks of saying no on the telephone, he said, "Don't you at least owe me the courtesy of a personal visit?" Now, if Welch wants your firstborn, by the end of the day you'll be childless.

I went in to the meeting with several reasons why I shouldn't take the job [to run Crotonville]. As I left Welch's office, I had a cognitive memory of those reasons, but that's all: I didn't want to be controlled; I wanted academic freedom. He took those reasons and shredded them.

When I became a full-timer, somebody gave me a plaque that read: "Life can be tragic. You're here today and here tomorrow." I never got worried, though. Welch woke me up to my own new intuition of how a company can be more advantageous to ideas—and meaningful to me personally—than academe. I knew that the character of my career would change from one where everything is set in stone to one that is *experimental*. You get to see how things end. Your life—and the life of the ideas you're working with—is binding. In academe, you can't put in a new course until it's accredited; the accreditation process takes a year. In private industry, everything was quick: Launch and learn, get good ideas out into the workplace, take chances. For example, at Crotonville I introduced a new idea about how to address deflation in eight days for sixty-five of the organization's top people. They then went back and experimented around this idea to find ways to make it happen.

The idea came out of the economic climate, but it had leadership support. Welch put out the word, "None of us have ever managed in a period when hard assets lost value over time. I want the head of sourcing of every business [to hear this idea at Crotonville]. I want the CFO of every business there—and if it's a manufacturing business bring in the head of manufacturing, otherwise invite the head IT guy."

You're not an economist, so how did you know that this was the right idea, and moreover, did you know how to link this idea to your organization?

I talked to people who knew what the customer should be—starting at the top. Jack said, "This idea is going to change the way we price, the way we market, the way we think of cycle time. Inventory now has a whole new meaning. It will change the way we write a contract, a subcontract, a five- versus a ten-year contract. . . . "

Then I ran it through my network in and outside of GE. I asked which industries "live like that now." I didn't find industries quite like that, but I found countries that were wildly inflationary, whose businesses closed up every afternoon to mark up their prices for the next day.

I was able to gain quick feedback about how to present the idea to these sixty-five executives. And I was then able to gain feedback from them. Gaining quick feedback and translating it into action and results is what advocating ideas is all about.

It sounds as though this idea was very much necessitated by, and a product of, the times. Were most of the ideas you advocated at GE this way?

Yes, but some ideas had a longer cycle time in the organization. I advocated Work-Out—an idea that has to do with participation and empowerment—for five years. There were constantly ideas around organizational structure, especially around how to create flat designs. We introduced ideas around heuristics, like [the idea that] there should be no more than five levels between the new hire and the head of the company. We introduced ideas around chain of command, span

of control. We introduced ideas about how to create synergies
. . . ideas about how to get out of our silos . . . ideas about
how to grow without becoming bureaucratic.

It is about balancing *a constant challenge to the status quo*
with *systems and measurements*. How do you reward people
for bringing bad news, for taking risk? How do you build di-
agnostics around this? In advocating ideas, it's important
never to confuse the edge of the ditch with the horizon.

How do you communicate an idea without diluting it?

I just see the world as simple concepts that respond to important problems. Here's a problem I'm thinking about
right now: At Goldman Sachs we want people to do cross-
divisional marketing. But all the rewards come from divisional marketing. My simple concept: Incentives such as
money supply people with energy.

The most transformational communication tool I ever used
at GE was $Q \times A = E$, the old Norman Maier formula. Quality times acceptance equals effectiveness. It affects the way
even high-level strategic ideas should be communicated. I
said to executives, "What if you guys build high-quality refrigerators nobody buys and you call them inventory? That's a
bad thing. What if you produce high-quality strategies and
everybody hates them? Why is that a good thing? Look how
you market to your external clients. You wouldn't say to your
customer, 'Effective Monday, buy it!' Who would advertise
that way?" But, inside GE, executives were marketing their
strategic ideas that way.

Welch would spend hours formulating and reformatting
his strategy. But he wouldn't spend two minutes on how to
sell the idea. His quartiling of people, his vitality curve—let's
fire the bottom ten percent—people hated those ideas. It
wasn't about Q; it was about A—about getting acceptance. I
brought him very simple models about how to gain acceptance for his ideas. Some think the ideal is *to seem impressive,*

to show an idea as a three-by-three when they could do it as a two-by-two. For me, the ideal is simplicity.

So this approach carried over into the way you evaluated new ideas and brought them into the firm?

Part of my job as CLO [chief learning officer] was to break down boundaries, penetrate the outside walls with new ideas. I constantly read. But ideas came in from lots of places. Vic Vroom [an organizational behavior professor at Yale] would come to Crotonville to talk about a leadership model based on fuzzy logic. Ram Charan [a leadership consultant] would come in and talk.

Ideas would come in through Welch as well. He got fascinated with the leadership development and mentoring stuff at PepsiCo and asked me to look into it. Another time, he was doing a customer visit and found a guy at American Standard (which makes urinals) who operated with no working capital. There was an idea! Six Sigma came in because Jack was having heart surgery and couldn't kill it. Six Sigma came in through a side door: George Fisher [CEO of Motorola and Kodak] initially came in and recommended it and Jack had continually said no—that the detailed regimentation of the Six Sigma approach wasn't right for GE. At the only meeting . . . of the corporate council [Welch ever missed], Larry Bossidy came in as a guest. (He had just started at AlliedSignal.) He said the one thing no one else could say: "If you guys do Six Sigma, you'll write the book!" There was so much excitement that even Welch couldn't stop it. Granted, Welch became an apostle, then went out and led it. But that idea came in through a side door.

So, yes, I'd bring in new ideas all of the time. Maybe more importantly, however, I had to create a life for good ideas—regardless of where they came from. Look at it this way: The human body needs a new kidney to stay alive; then the immune system kicks in fraudulently and rejects it.

Organizations do that too often. They reject the ideas they need to stay alive. My value-add was to be a source of ideas— but not the only one—and to prevent this rejection.

How were you able to prevent your organization from wrong-fully rejecting a good idea?

You know the little old man with the stamp who can go around your town and label a building or statue or park a his-torical standard? Crotonville could label something an official corporate experiment—what GE called popcorn stands. Of course, they would start out in practice first; I'd label them later. A manager working for a mortgage loan guarantee firm (a GE business) in New York wanted me to come and validate one of her experiments as a best practice. Jim Champy had al-ready called it the best white-collar application of reengineer-ing he had ever seen. But she said, "I work for Gary Wendt [then the head of GE Capital]. Gary is not the most patient man. My numbers are marginal. I'm afraid he's going to kill the idea and the business." I went down there and liked what was going on. I called Gary and told him that he had a great popcorn stand [i.e., corporate experiment] going on in one of his businesses. Now, if that business was losing a lot of money, Gary would still have killed the business. But at the margin, he would be likely to let it run for a while.

Every organization has natural experiments. But if you don't think of it that way and transfer this knowledge into deep action, it won't prosper. At GE this was my protective layer. Labeling the idea as a formal experiment can keep a good idea in place longer and offer damage control if it hap-pens not to work.

You were credentialed, you had legitimization, you had incred-ible support from the CEO at GE, you had a title—chief learn-ing officer—you had a corporate imprimatur. Was there any-thing else that explains your success?

I hated failure. But I understood that if you ruthlessly sup-
press failure, you drive it underground. You've got to learn
from failure, but you cannot do that if it's denied. You can't
fail in large ways, for example, in a business where you make
all your money. But you can afford to fail while experiment-
ing. Insofar as the organization learns—even from failure—it
becomes stronger.

*Is it possible to replicate the kind of imprimatur that GE gave
you in other firms?*
Well, Goldman Sachs has devised a structure, and created a
cache, for "Pine Street" (named after the birthplace of the
firm) to be successful, and I benefit from the same level of top
management that I had in GE.

*There must be differences between these two elite firms,
though.*
At GE, leadership and management were revered. At the end
of the day, a leader at GE could say, "I don't know how to
make a jet engine. Why should I? I've got people who can do
that." At Goldman, if Bob Steele, for example, said, "I don't
understand the equities business," he would lose credibility.
They believe that expertise makes good leadership. Management is not your day job; managers are "producer-managers."
Here your job is to be with clients.

This requires a fundamentally new orientation and challenge for me: At GE they moved potential leaders across
boundaries. The guy who ran the small appliances business,
Bob Wright, became the head of GE Capital, then head of
NBC. *Variety* magazine initially laughed at the notion of a
pots-and-pans guy running NBC. He became the most successful TV executive of his day. He knows about management, how to hire and retain talent, how to run a meeting,
and so on. In investment banks, bankers are the mainly the
ones who move from their silos to other divisions, or to run

the firm. If you're in fixed income, in equities or a trader, you generally stay in your silo.

At GE, how did you align ideas with what management cared about? Was it about getting the language right?

Yes, that is a crucial point. I'd find ways of having good information flows come to me. I would attend meetings and listen to what GE's Corporate Executive Council had to say. I was a member of the corporate staff review. I was able to hear what the organization's priorities were and thereby integrate the ideas. The top priority was for the organization to become boundaryless [a riff on efficiency and effectiveness]. So becoming boundaryless was the raison d'être for all ideas I advocated.

Any idea I advocated had to help penetrate one of three boundaries. Work-Out, for example, is about moving empowerment down into lower levels. Six Sigma is about breaking down inside and outside walls. The conceptual language of becoming boundaryless was always a starting point. The concept of boundarylessness serves as a powerful integrator. It's about helping the organization assimilate the change rather than rejecting it. It's similar elsewhere.

Bad consultants say that people can only keep two ideas in mind at a time. That is horrible advice; if your competitor can work with nine ideas at a time, you will lose. So, for example, the CEO might have to work with thirteen new ideas, the CFO ten, and the guy in the mailroom only one. But collectively, all twenty-four ideas would have to be assimilated and used to good advantage.

At GE the language of boundarylessness was the integrator. It is a matter of communication. If you hear about reengineering or mass customization, you need to be able to explain how it makes the company more boundaryless. Don't ever bring in an idea that feels disconnected.

You're talking about nurturing a paradox: Add more ideas, but subtract from the overall workload?

Right. But it can be unraveled by looking at the interpretation process. If an idea is (rhetorically) framed around something that a manager already knows and cares about, much of the intellectual workload is already done. You make ideas successful by not adding to workload.

Are you happy you spent your life working with business ideas?

Yes. And the key to being able to say yes is being able to learn in every job you take.

A SELECT SURVEY OF BUSINESS AND MANAGEMENT IDEAS

Activity-based costing[1]
Activity value analysis
Adaptive enterprises
Artificial Intelligence
Attention management
Balanced scorecard
Benchmarking
Brainstorming
Brand management
Business modeling
Cannibalization
Centralization/
  decentralization
Change management
Chaos/complexity
Competitive
  intelligence
Complex adaptive
  systems
Concurrent engineering
Conglomeration
Continuous
  improvement

Co-opetition
Core capabilities
Core competence
Corporate culture
Cost-benefit analysis
Creative destruction
Crisis management
Critical-path analysis
Cross-selling
Customer relationship
  management (CRM)
Customer satisfaction
De-layering
Decision trees
Diversification
Double-loop learning
Downsizing
e-Commerce
e-Marketplaces
Economic value
  analysis (EVA)
Economies of
  scale/scope

Electronic data
  interchange (EDI)
Empowerment
Enterprise systems
Entrepreneurship
Evolutionary modeling
Excellence
Experience curves
Experience economy
Five forces analysis
Flat organizations
Franchising
Game theory
Globalization
Growth/share matrix
Hawthorne effect
Hierarchy of needs
Horizontal
  organization
Information ecology
Information
  management
Intellectual capitalism

Intellectual property
  management
Interorganizational
  systems
Intrapreneurship
Just-in-time delivery
Keiretsu
Knowledge
  management
Lead user analysis
Leadership
Lean production
Learning organizations
Lifetime customer
  value
Loyalty management
Management by
  objectives
Management by
  walking around
Managerial grid
Marketing myopia
Mass customization
Mass production
Matrix management
Mentoring
Mission statements
One-minute managing
Open-book
  management
Operations research
Organizational ecology

Outsourcing
Paradigms
Pay-for-performance
Permission marketing
Portfolio analysis
Portfolio management
Process improvement
Product life cycles
Profit pools
Prototyping
Quality circles
Quality of work life
Real options
Reengineering
Resource-based
  strategy
Restructuring
S-curves
Satisficing
Scenario planning
Scientific management
Scientific retailing
Segmentation
Services
Seven S model
Simulation
Six Sigma
Social capital
Sociotechnical systems
Spans of control
Strategic alignment
Strategic business units

Strategic planning
Strengths, weaknesses,
  opportunities,
  threats (SWOT)
  analysis
Succession planning
Supply chain
  management
Synergy
Systems dynamics
T groups
Teams
Technology transfer
Theories X and Y
Theory Z
Time-based
  competition
Total quality
  management (TQM)
Unbundling
Value chain
Value disciplines
Value migration
Value proposition
Vertical/horizontal
  integration
Virtual organizations
Vision
War for talent
Wellness
Yield management
Zero-based budgeting

APPENDIX B

THE IDEA PRACTITIONERS

Mohi Ahmed, Fujitsu Micro-
electronics
Patti Anklam, Nortel
Dave Barrow, British Petroleum (BP)
Lawrence Baxter, Wachovia
Corporation
Carol Bekar, Bristol-Myers Squibb
Alex Bennet, U.S. Navy (formerly)
Lowell Bryan, McKinsey &
Company
Mike Burtha, Johnson & Johnson
Dave Clarke, American Red Cross
Chris Collison, BP (formerly)
Susan Conway, Microsoft
John Cross, BP (formerly)
Martin Curley, Intel
Lynn Dann, Eastman Kodak
Company
Howard Dean, KPMG
Steve Denning, The World Bank
(formerly)
Tony DiMarco, Naviquest

John Egan, Dell Computer
Barcy Fox, Russell Reynolds
Associates
Ted Graham, Hewitt Associates
Giora Hadar, Federal Aviation
Administration
Sue Hanley, Plural (now part of Dell)
Chris Hoenig, U.S. General Account-
ing Office (formerly)
Dan Holtshouse, Xerox
June Huber, U.S. General Services
Administration
Larry Huston, Procter & Gamble
Steve Kerr, Goldman Sachs
James Kinney, Kraft Foods
Joel Kurtzman,
PricewaterhouseCoopers
Mark Maletz, Babson
Blythe McGarvie, BIC
Joe McCrea, Office of the E-envoy,
United Kingdom
Gene Meieran, Intel

Joel Miller, Eli Lilly and Company
Manuela Mueller, Siemens
Vik Muznieks, Nortel
Valerie Norton, ING Barings Group
John M. Old, Texaco (formerly)
Duncan Onyango, Abbey National
Kate Owen, BP
Antonella Padova, Whirlpool
(formerly)
Josh Plaskoff, Eli Lilly and Company
James L. Poage, Volpe Center, U.S.
Department of Transportation
Dave Pollard, Ernst & Young
John Powell, Hewitt Associates
Ted Richman, Xerox (now Harris
Interactive)
Shelley Rosen, McDonald's

Aliana Rozenek, Canadian Imperial
Bank of Commerce
Barbara Saidel, Russell Reynolds
Associates
Hubert Saint-Onge, Clarica
(formerly)
Charles Seeley, Intel
Sanjiv Sidhu, i2 Technologies
Chuck Sieloff, Institute for the
Future (formerly of Hewlett-
Packard)
Reuben Slone, Whirlpool
Debbie Smith, State Street Bank and
Trust Co.
Dave Snowden, IBM
Mitzi Wertheim, U.S. Center of
Naval Analysis

APPENDIX C

THE TOP TWO HUNDRED BUSINESS GURUS

Guru Rank	Name	Google Hits	Google Hit Ranking	SSCI Citations	SSCI Rank	Media Mentions	Media Rank	Sum of Ranks
1	Michael Porter	18,536	13	3,129	2	2,338	8	23
2	Tom Peters	33,364	6	883	25	2,209	7	38
3	Robert Reich	31,488	7	791	27	6,304	5	39
4	Peter Drucker	49,760	2	1,202	15	590	33	60
5	Gary S. Becker	9,355	32	3,912	1	682	26	59
6	Peter Senge	18,290	14	1,312	12	585	34	60
7	Gary Hamel	9,624	30	1,065	18	772	22	70
8	Alvin Toffler	44,670	3	352	63	2,848	6	72
9	Hal Varian	13,550	19	912	23	454	43	85
9	Daniel Goleman	10,603	28	603	36	779	21	85
11	Rosabeth Moss Kanter	7,617	41	1,357	10	545	37	88
12	Ronald Coase	7,117	42	1,534	7	338	51	100
12	Lester Thurow	8,510	36	532	40	708	24	100
14	Charles Handy	8,022	37	528	41	625	29	107
15	Paul Romer	4,666	57	1,342	11	463	42	110
16	Henry Mintzberg	5,440	52	1,591	6	289	57	115
16	Stephen Covey	20,660	10	184	96	2,099	9	115
18	Michael Hammer	6,372	47	775	29	487	40	116
19	Bill Gates	510,059	1	127	118	81,600	1	120
20	Warren Bennis	10,030	29	393	56	558	36	121
21	Jeffrey Pfeffer	4,511	60	1,870	4	273	60	124
22	Philip Kotler	8,660	34	826	26	243	66	126
23	Robert C. Merton	3,250	84	1,057	19	609	31	134
24	C. K. Prahalad	6,910	44	1,011	21	208	76	141
24	Thomas H. Davenport	6,763	45	647	34	270	62	141
26	Don Tapscott	12,160	21	192	94	626	28	143
27	Malcolm Gladwell	12,087	22	162	104	780	20	146
28	John Seely Brown	7,688	40	357	62	425	45	147
29	George Gilder	13,850	18	121	119	897	14	151

Guru Rank	Name	Google Hits	Google Hit Ranking	SSCI Citations	SSCI Rank	Media Mentions	Media Rank	Sum of Ranks
30	Kevin Kelly	11,865	24	156	106	703	25	155
30	Chris Argyris	5,120	54	1,302	13	157	88	155
32	Esther Dyson	19,016	11	79	137	1,812	11	159
33	Robert Kaplan	4,454	61	524	44	307	56	161
34	Edward DeBono	11,338	26	138	114	745	23	163
34	Jack Welch	38,836	4	49	156	11,703	3	163
36	John Kotter	6,130	49	456	49	223	73	171
37	Ken Blanchard	16,957	15	74	141	824	18	174
38	Edward Tufte	10,810	27	386	57	140	96	180
39	Kenichi Ohmae	4,597	58	307	70	327	54	182
40	James MacGregor Burns	4,558	59	283	75	382	49	183
41	Alfred Chandler	2,728	95	1,046	20	227	69	184
41	Edgar Schein	5,423	53	1,534	7	92	124	184
43	Sumantra Ghoshal	4,132	68	498	47	225	71	186
44	Myron S. Scholes	3,464	81	197	91	829	16	188
45	Richard Branson	30,750	8	14	180	26,473	2	190
46	Anthony Robbins	15,845	16	34	162	851	15	193
46	Michael Dell	28,500	9	14	180	9,475	4	193
48	James March	3,109	87	1,809	5	129	102	194
49	Clayton Christensen	4,228	65	237	87	443	44	196
50	John Naisbitt	6,580	46	148	109	411	47	202
51	Don Peppers	13,925	17	82	134	333	53	204
52	David Teece	2,152	109	1,135	17	181	80	206
53	Thomas Stewart	5,507	50	302	72	160	87	209
54	Andrew S. Grove	7,040	43	48	157	2,000	10	210
54	Ed Lawler	2,034	118	789	28	251	64	210
56	Geert Hofstede	2,961	90	2,044	3	98	119	212
57	Ikujiro Nonaka	3,139	85	917	22	115	106	213
58	Patricia Seybold	11,716	25	18	172	825	17	214
59	Robert Sutton	2,346	104	513	45	233	67	216
60	Geoffrey A. Moore	8,876	33	71	145	511	39	217
60	Larry Bossidy	36,928	5	0	200	1,396	12	217
62	David Norton	4,266	64	148	109	368	50	223
63	Noel Tichy	3,121	86	260	80	268	63	229
63	Richard Nelson	2,744	93	885	24	108	112	229
65	Karl Weick	2,275	106	1,446	9	96	121	236
66	Gareth Morgan	4,355	63	714	30	62	147	240
66	Bob Metcalfe	8,012	38	27	167	581	35	240
68	Robert Axelrod	3,543	78	1,297	14	60	150	242
69	John Hagel	4,417	62	134	116	248	65	243
70	James C. Collins	2,539	99	161	105	471	41	245
70	Spencer Johnson	18,934	12	18	172	271	61	245
72	Guy Kawasaki	9,472	31	10	185	610	30	246
73	Joseph Juran	2,316	105	404	54	157	88	247
73	Fred Reichheld	2,850	91	238	86	226	70	247
73	Martha Rogers	7,830	39	37	160	384	48	247
76	James Champy	4,217	66	101	125	287	58	249
76	Nitin Nohria	2,581	97	399	55	139	97	249
78	Margaret J. Wheatley	5,490	51	185	95	114	107	253
79	James Brian Quinn	3,346	82	570	37	68	141	260
80	Eliyahu Goldratt	4,878	56	98	127	173	83	266
81	Ted Levitt	2,230	108	317	68	154	92	268
82	Michael Schrage	3,759	74	82	134	232	68	276
83	Brian Arthur	3,493	80	657	33	42	166	279
84	Jerry Porras	3,988	69	86	133	185	79	281
85	Michael Useem	1,902	122	281	76	165	86	284
86	Thomas M. Siebel	3,503	79	6	191	809	19	289

Guru Rank	Name	Google Hits	Google Hit Ranking	SSCI Citations	SSCI Rank	Media Mentions	Media Rank	Sum of Ranks
87	Nicholas Negroponte	13,320	20	269	78	21	193	291
88	Terrence Deal	3,786	73	250	84	74	135	292
89	Barry Nalebuff	2,388	102	253	82	110	110	294
89	Stan Davis	3,603	76	166	102	101	116	294
91	Kathleen Eisenhardt	1,095	155	1,185	16	88	125	296
92	Christopher A. Bartlett	1,059	158	509	46	153	93	297
92	Baruch Lev	1,899	123	166	102	224	72	297
92	David Shenk	3,004	88	39	158	338	51	297
95	Chris Locke	8,522	35	9	186	193	78	299
95	Percy Barnevik	3,306	83	7	189	646	27	299
97	Jay Alden Conger	1,679	135	347	64	111	108	307
97	Peter Keen	3,626	75	289	73	55	159	307
99	Larry Prusak	3,872	70	75	139	135	100	309
100	David Weinberger	6,338	48	9	186	196	77	311
101	N. Venkatraman	1,794	131	558	38	67	143	312
102	Kim Clark	311	196	608	35	176	81	312
103	Karl Albrecht	2,767	92	28	166	318	55	313
104	Fons Trompenaars	1,917	121	143	111	174	82	314
105	Sidney Winter	1,590	139	373	60	101	116	315
105	Jon R. Katzenbach	2,982	89	179	98	80	128	315
107	Chris Meyer	3,801	71	31	163	155	90	324
108	Richard Saul Wurman	4,926	55	24	169	129	102	326
109	Seth Godin	11,990	23	17	176	77	131	330
110	John Kay	951	166	88	130	542	38	334
110	William Ouchi	987	160	548	39	74	135	334
112	Ram Charan	3,558	77	51	154	124	104	335
113	Frances Cairncross	1,401	145	155	107	166	85	337
114	Bruce Kogut	1,380	146	706	31	51	160	337
115	David Nadler	1,688	134	241	85	96	121	340
116	Paul Strassmann	2,385	103	72	143	139	97	343
117	Michael Earl	2,117	112	268	79	59	153	344
118	Etienne Wenger	2,731	94	257	81	40	172	347
118	Robert Eccles	1,046	159	274	77	109	111	347
118	James O'Toole	1,616	136	1	198	910	13	347
121	John Harvey Jones	1,703	133	12	184	596	32	349
122	Yves Doz	1,164	151	312	69	77	131	351
123	Susan A. Mohrman	2,422	101	178	99	59	153	353
124	Arie De Geus	1,724	132	112	122	132	101	355
125	Philip Evans	2,578	98	31	163	143	94	355
126	Peter Schwartz	3,799	72	22	170	106	113	355
127	Richard D'Aveni	1,811	129	347	64	42	166	359
128	Robert Waterman	1,430	143	64	146	216	74	363
129	Dorothy Leonard	2,131	110	138	114	68	141	365
130	Stewart Clegg	753	178	380	59	78	129	366
131	David Garvin	1,086	156	498	47	42	166	369
132	George Stalk	1,455	142	324	67	48	163	372
132	Alan Webber	2,055	117	30	165	155	90	372
134	Liam Fahey	2,460	100	104	124	60	150	374
135	Jay Galbraith	1,809	130	345	66	34	179	375
136	Shoshana Zuboff	1,556	140	386	57	34	179	376
137	John Child	1,422	144	453	50	31	183	377
138	Watts Wacker	1,880	124	1	198	281	59	381
139	Karl Erik Sveiby	2,129	111	75	139	76	133	383
140	Stafford Beer	2,066	115	284	74	20	195	384
141	B. Joseph Pine II	1,337	148	168	101	70	138	387
142	John Henderson	2,233	107	252	83	12	198	388
143	Michael Treacy	2,105	113	72	143	76	133	389

Guru Rank	Name	Google Hits	Google Hit Ranking	SSCI Citations	SSCI Rank	Media Mentions	Media Rank	Sum of Ranks
143	Andrew M. Pettigrew	879	169	525	43	35	177	389
145	Russ Ackoff	428	192	416	53	64	145	390
146	Jeffrey A. Sonnenfeld	401	193	110	123	215	75	391
147	David Ulrich	2,067	114	199	90	24	189	393
148	Leif Edvinsson	1,956	119	57	151	85	126	396
149	Jay Lorsch	585	189	154	108	118	105	402
150	Charles Hampden-Turner	1,612	137	114	120	62	147	404
150	John Kao	1,493	141	60	149	104	114	404
152	Ronald Burt	615	187	688	32	25	187	406
153	Stephen Barley	668	184	528	41	31	183	408
154	Jeff Rayport	889	167	95	128	101	116	411
155	Richard Foster	694	181	62	147	170	84	412
156	Charles Leadbeater	1,227	150	59	150	104	114	414
157	Fred Wiersema	2,057	116	14	180	97	120	416
158	Paul S. Adler	817	173	418	52	22	192	417
158	Marshall Goldsmith	4,135	67	2	194	58	156	417
160	Richard J. Schonberger	806	175	304	71	39	173	419
161	Richard Pascale	970	164	195	93	48	163	420
162	Robert Hayes	706	180	426	51	23	190	421
162	Michael Cohen	817	173	360	61	25	187	421
164	Adam Brandenburger	985	161	184	96	42	166	423
164	Manfred Kets de Vries	859	170	177	100	59	153	423
164	Patrick M. Lencioni	2,720	96	5	192	74	135	423
167	John Sviokla	1,594	138	88	130	58	156	424
168	Mohanbir Sawhney	1,304	149	13	183	142	95	427
169	W. Chan Kim	286	197	237	87	66	144	428
170	Joel Kurtzman	976	163	17	176	136	99	438
171	Lucy Kellaway	215	199	2	194	416	46	439
172	Douglas K. Smith	1,842	126	26	168	62	147	441
173	Gifford Pinchot	1,920	120	56	152	41	171	443
173	Lee G. Bolman	1,838	127	50	155	50	161	443
175	Chunka Mui	1,853	125	2	194	83	127	446
176	Andrew Campbell	979	162	61	148	70	138	448
177	Joseph L. Bower	333	195	207	89	42	166	450
178	Richard Nolan	1,125	154	99	126	37	176	456
178	Nancy M. Dixon	1,834	128	73	142	30	186	456
180	Harold Leavitt	828	171	140	112	32	181	464
181	Steve Kerr	658	186	197	91	23	190	467
182	Michael Maccoby	825	172	56	152	64	145	469
182	James F. Moore	666	185	35	161	93	123	469
184	Richard Boyatzis	767	177	113	121	35	177	475
185	Nancy Koehn	672	183	7	189	111	108	480
186	Rashi H. Glazer	463	191	130	117	38	174	482
187	Marvin R. Weisbord	1,154	152	76	138	11	199	489
188	Marvin Bower	1,071	157	18	172	49	162	491
189	Ricardo Semler	775	176	16	178	70	138	492
189	Lowell Bryan	962	165	20	171	58	156	492
191	Elliott Jaques	518	190	139	113	21	193	496
192	Francis Gouillart	214	200	18	172	78	129	501
193	David Feeny	383	194	88	130	31	183	507
194	H. Thomas Johnson	684	182	90	129	16	197	508
195	G. Bennett Stewart	586	188	38	159	47	165	512
196	Jack Stack	745	179	9	186	60	150	515
197	Stephen Denning	882	168	15	179	38	174	521
198	Allan Kennedy	1,148	153	2	194	32	181	528
199	Renée Mauborgne	217	198	81	136	10	200	534
200	Adrian Slywotsky	1,352	147	4	193	19	196	536

NOTES

Preface

1. Richard A. Posner, *Public Intellectuals: A Study of Decline* (Cambridge: Harvard University Press, 2001)

Chapter 1

1. The quote and much other information about Westinghouse comes from Steve Massey, "Who Killed Westinghouse?" *Pittsburgh Post-Gazette,* 1998 (series of articles), available at < www.postgazette.com/westinghouse >.

2. GE quotations are from Robert G. Eccles and Nitin Nohria, *Beyond the Hype: Rediscovering the Essence of Management* (Boston: Harvard Business School Press, 1992), 21–22. Many of Ralph Cordiner's ideas are laid out in his book, *New Frontiers for Professional Managers* (New York: McGraw-Hill, 1956).

3. Christopher A. Bartlett and Meg Glinska, "GE's Digital Revolution: Redefining the E in GE," Case 9-399-055 (Boston: Harvard Business School, 2002).

4. Ibid.

5. Andrea Gabor, "Anticipating Welch on Welch," *New York Times,* 29 November 2000.

6. See, for example, Noel Tichy and Stratford Sherman, *Control Your Destiny or Someone Else Will* (New York: HarperBusiness, 1994).

7. David Ulrich, Steve Kerr, and Ron Ashkenas, *The GE Work-Out* (New York: McGraw-Hill, 2002).

8. Ibid., 9.

9. Ronald N. Ashkenas, Dave Ulrich, Todd Jick, and Steve Kerr, eds., *The Boundaryless Organization* (New York: Wiley, 1995).

10. These figures about GE are from Eileen C. Shapiro, *Fad Surfing in the Boardroom: Reclaiming the Courage to Manage in the Age of Instant Answers* (Cambridge, MA: Perseus, 1995), 193.

11. Barry M. Staw and Lisa Epstein, "What Bandwagons Bring: Effects of Popular Management Techniques on Corporate Performance, Reputation and CEO Pay," *Administrative Science Quarterly* 45 (2000): 523–556.

12. Ernst & Young LLP, "Measures That Matter," report from the Center for Business Innovation (Cambridge, MA: Ernst & Young LLP, 1996).

13. Nitin Nohria and Sandy E. Green, "Efficiency and Legitimacy: The Adoption of TQM by Large Industrial Corporations," working paper 96-055, Harvard Business School, Boston, 1996.

14. John Micklethwait and Adrien Wooldridge, *The Witch Doctors* (New York: Times Books, 1996).

15. Kennedy Information Research Group, Peterborough, NH, "The Global Management Consulting Market: Key Data, Forecasts and Trends," research report, 2002.

Chapter 2

1. Stephen Denning, *The Springboard: How Storytelling Ignites Action in Knowledge-Era Organizations* (Medford, MA: Butterworth-Heinemann, 2000).

2. Christopher A. Bartlett and Meg Glinska, "GE's Digital Revolution: Redefining the E in GE," Case 9-399-055 (Boston: Harvard Business School, 2002).

3. The narrative in this chapter comes from an interview, but Steve Denning's reflections on the power of stories in creating change are described in Denning, *The Springboard*.

4. The source of this quip was Warren McFarlan at Harvard Business School. We're not sure if he made it up, but it's consistent with his wit and wisdom.

5. Tracy Mayor, "Red Light, Green Light: Case Files," *CIO*, 1 October 2001, < www.cio.com/archive/100101/red.html >.

Chapter 3

1. Darrell K. Rigby, Bain & Company online publication, "Executives Vote for 'Tried and True' Techniques to Navigate Downturn," < http://www.bain .com/bainweb/publications/Written_By_Bain_detail.asp?article_id = 5621 >.

2. Thomas H. Davenport, *Mission Critical: Realizing the Promise of Enterprise Systems* (Boston: Harvard Business School Press, 2000).

3. Nitin Nohria et al., *Changing Fortunes: Remaking the Industrial Corporation* (New York: Wiley, 2002).

4. Barbara Ettorre, "What's the Next Business Buzzword?" *Management Review* 86, no. 8 (1997): 33–35.

5. J. Whitney and D. Tesone, "Management Fads: Emergence, Evolution, and Implications for Managers," *Academy of Management Executive* 15, no. 4 (2001): 124.

6. See, for example, John Micklethwait and Adrien Wooldridge, *The Witch Doctors* (New York: Times Books, 1996); Eileen C. Shapiro, *Fad Surfing in the Boardroom: Reclaiming the Courage to Manage in the Age of Instant Answers* (Cambridge, MA: Perseus, 1995); Robert E. Cole, *Managing Quality Fads* (Oxford: Oxford University Press, 1999); Richard G. Hamermesh, *Fad-Free Management: The Six Principles That Drive Successful Companies and Their Leaders* (Santa Monica, CA: Knowledge Exchange, 1996).

7. Shapiro, *Fad Surfing*, 1.

8. Richard T. Pascale, *Managing on the Edge* (New York: Touchstone Books, 1991).

9. *Harvard Business Review* 1, no.1 (1922): 1, quoted in Margaret C. Brindle and Peter N. Stearns, *Facing Up to Management Faddism* (Greenwich, CT: Quorum Books, 2001), 2.

10. Cole, *Managing Quality Fads*, 235.

11. Thomas H. Davenport, *Process Innovation: Reengineering Work Through Information Technology* (Boston: Harvard Business School Press, 1993): 14–15.

12. Brindle and Stearns, *Facing Up to Management Faddism*, 52.

13. Suzy Wetlaufer, "The Business Case Against Revolution: An Interview with Nestlé's Peter Brabeck," *Harvard Business Review* (February 2001): 114.

Chapter 4

1. Frederick W. Taylor, *Principles of Scientific Management* (New York: Harper, 1911), 29.

2. Gary Hamel and C. K. Prahalad, "The Core Competence of the Corporation," *Harvard Business Review*, May–June 1990.

3. Edith Penrose, *The Theory of the Firm*, 3d ed. (New York: Oxford University Press, 1999).

4. Gary Hamel, *Leading the Revolution* (Boston: Harvard Business School Press, 2000), 11.

5. The intellectual history of the balanced-scorecard idea is documented in great detail on Schneiderman's Web site at < www.schneiderman.com >.

6. Timothy Clark and David Greatbach, "Collaborative Relationships in the Creation and Fashioning of Management Ideas: Gurus, Editors, and Managers,"

in *Management Consulting: Emergence and Dynamics of a Knowledge Industry,* ed. M. Kipping and L. Engwall (New York: Oxford University Press, 2002), 140.

7. The number of conferences in the United States is taken from correspondence with Jaime Gonzalez, CEO of allconferences.net, a Web site that attempts to list all U.S. conferences.

8. Richard A. Posner, *Public Intellectuals: A Study of Decline* (Cambridge: Harvard University Press, 2002).

9. Unlike Posner, we excluded from our list any business gurus who are no longer alive.

10. Robert I. Sutton, "Why Managers Need Scholarly Research," working paper, Stanford Department of Management Science and Engineering, March 2000, 4.

11. Margarete Arndt et al., "Presenting Structural Innovation in an Institutional Environment: Hospitals' Use of Impression Management," *Administrative Science Quarterly* 45, no. 3 (2000): 494–522.

12. Warren G. Bennis, *On Becoming a Leader* (Cambridge, MA: Perseus, 1994); and Warren G. Bennis and Robert J. Thomas, *Geeks and Geezers: How Era, Values, and Defining Moments Shape Leaders* (Boston: Harvard Business School Press, 2002).

13. Frederick F. Reichheld, *The Loyalty Effect: The Hidden Force Behind Growth, Profits, and Lasting Value* (Boston: Harvard Business School Press, 1996); and Frederick F. Reichheld, *Loyalty Rules! How Leaders Build Lasting Relationships in the Digital Age* (Boston: Harvard Business School Press, 2001).

14. Charles Perrow, *Complex Organizations* (New York: McGraw-Hill, 1986), 65.

15. For more on Barnard's current influence, see Oliver Williamson, ed., *Organization Theory* (Oxford: Oxford University Press, 1995).

16. Chris Bartlett and Sumantra Ghoshal, *The Individualized Corporation* (New York: HarperBusiness, 1999).

17. Tom Stewart, "Brainpower: How Intellectual Capital Is Becoming America's Most Important Asset," *Fortune,* 3 June 1991, 44.

Chapter 5

1. This section is greatly influenced by Paul DiMaggio and Walter W. Powell, "The Iron Cage Revisited: Institutional Isomorphism and Collective Rationality," in *The New Institutionalism in Organizational Analysis,* ed. Paul DiMaggio and Walter W. Powell (Chicago: University of Chicago Press, 1991). In this highly influential article, organizational sociologists DiMaggio and Powell describe the various forces that assail and sway managers when they are choosing and buying ideas.

2. Lynne Zucker, "Institutional Theories of Organization," *Annual Review of Sociology* 13 (1978): 443–464.

3. Barry M. Staw and Lisa Epstein, "What Bandwagons Bring: Effects of Popular Management Techniques on Corporate Performance, Reputation and CEO Pay," *Administrative Science Quarterly* 45 (2000): 523–556.

4. For a discussion of the advice industry, see Paul DiMaggio, ed., *The Twenty-First Century Firm* (Princeton, NJ: Princeton University Press, 2001).

5. For a semi-whimsical estimate, see Donald McCloskey's article on persuasion, "One Quarter of GDP in Persuasion," *American Economic Review* 85, no. 2 (1995).

6. See, for example, Stephen Denning, *The Springboard: How Storytelling Ignites Action in Knowledge-Era Organizations* (Medford, MA: Butterworth-Heinemann, 2000); Roger S. Schank, *Tell Me a Story: Narrative and Intelligence (Rethinking Theory)* (Evanston, IL: Northwestern University Press, 1995).

7. See Albert Bates Lord et al., *The Singer of Tales* (Cambridge: Harvard University Press, 2000).

8. Jim Collins, *Good to Great: Why Some Companies Make the Leap . . . and Others Don't* (New York: HarperBusiness, 2001), 256.

Chapter 6

1. David Collins, *Management Fads and Buzzwords: Critical-Practical Perspectives* (London: Routledge, 2000), 127.

2. There have been several noteworthy bibliometric and other empirical studies examining the correlations between the production of certain types of management ideas (or rhetorics) and exogenouos environmental influences. See Eric Abrahamson, "Management Fashion: Lifecycles, Triggers, and Collective Learning Processes," *Administrative Science Quarterly* 44, no. 4 (1999); Eric Abrahamson, "The Emergence and Prevalence of Employee Management Rhetorics: The Effects of Long Waves, Labor Unions, and Turnover, 1875–1992," *Academy of Management Journal* 40, no. 3 (1997); Eric Abrahamson, "Management Fashion; Management Fads," *Academy of Management Review* 21, no. 1 (1996); Eric Abrahamson and Charles Fombrun, "Macrocultures: Determinants and Consequences," *Academy of Management Review* 19, no. 4 (1994); Paula Carson et al., "A Historical Perspective on Fad Adoption and Abandonment," *Journal of Management History* 5, no. 6 (1999); and Timothy Clark and Graeme Salaman, "Telling Tales," *Journal of Management Studies* 35, no. 2 (1998).

3. Douglas Hayward, "Cracking the Midmarket," *Upside* 14, no. 6 (2002): 36–41.

4. Doug Smith, "Blown to Bits: How the New Economics of Information Transforms Strategy," *Consulting to Management* 13, no. 2 (2002): 61–62.

5. Janne Tienari, Sigrid Quack, and Hildegard Theobald, "Organizational Reforms, 'Ideal Workers' and Gender Orders: A Cross-Societal Comparison," *Organization Studies* 23, no. 2 (2002): 249–279.

6. Ed Lawler, interview by Ned Hamson, "Organizing for High Performance," *Journal for Quality and Participation* 24, no. 4 (2001): 14–19.

7. Margaret Langstaff, "Turning on a Dime," *Publishers Weekly*, 9 July 2001.

8. Thomas H. Davenport, *Process Innovation: Reengineering Work Through Information Technology* (Boston: Harvard Business School Press, 1993).

9. Thomas H. Davenport, "Coming Soon: The CKO," *Information Week*, 5 September 1994, 95.

Chapter 7

1. Thomas H. Davenport and James E. Short, "The New Industrial Engineering: Information Technology and Business Process Redesign," *Sloan Management Review* (summer 1990): 11.

2. Thomas H. Davenport, *Process Innovation: Reengineering Work Through Information Technology* (Boston: Harvard Business School Press, 1993).

3. George Stalk and Thomas M. Hout, *Competing Against Time* (New York: Free Press, 1990).

4. Paul Strassman, *The Politics of Information Management* (New Canaan, CT: Information Economics Press, 1994), 157.

5. Thomas H. Davenport, "The Fad That Forgot People," *Fast Company*, premiere issue (October 1995).

6. Michael Hammer and James A. Champy, *Reengineering the Corporation: A Manifesto for Business Revolution* (New York: HarperCollins, 1993).

7. Joseph B. White, "Re-Engineering Gurus Take Steps to Remodel Their Stalling Vehicles," *Wall Street Journal*, 26 November 1996.

8. Strassman, *The Politics of Information Management*, 234–236.

9. David Collins, *Management Fads and Buzzwords: Critical-Practical Perspectives* (London: Routledge, 2000), 254.

10. In addition to Collins's work, see, for example, Margaret C. Brindle and Peter N. Stearns, *Facing Up to Management Faddism* (Greenwich, CT: Quorum Books, 2001); John Micklethwait and Adrien Wooldridge, *The Witch Doctors* (New York: Times Books, 1996).

11. John Seely Brown and Paul Duguid, "Organizational Learning and Communities-of-Practice: Toward a Unified View of Working, Learning, and Innovation," *Organization Science* 2 (February 1991): 40–57. This is also an example of how sometimes very significant ideas originally show up in arcane places.

12. Hammer and Champy, *Reengineering the Corporation*.

13. Michael Hammer, "Process Management and the Future of Six Sigma," *Sloan Management Review* (winter 2002): 26–32.

14. Michael Hammer, *The Agenda: What Every Business Must Do to Dominate the Decade* (New York: Crown, 2001).

15. James Champy, *X-Engineering the Corporation* (New York: Warner Business Books, 2002).

Chapter 8

1. Much of the thinking that emerged from that program can found in Thomas H. Davenport (with Laurence Prusak), *Information Ecology* (Oxford: Oxford University Press, 1997).

2. Kenneth Arrow, "The Economic Implications of Learning by Doing," *Review of Economic Studies* 29 (June 1962): 153–173.

3. Daniel Bell, *The Coming of Post-Industrial Society* (New York: Basic Books, 1989).

4. Alvin Toffler, *Future Shock* (New York: Bantam Books, 1991).

5. Fritz Machlup, ed., *Information: Multidisciplinary Messages* (New York: Wiley, 1984).

6. Michael Polanyi, *The Tacit Dimension* (Gloucester, MA: Peter Smith Publishers, 1983); and Michael Polyanyi, *Personal Knowledge* (Chicago: University of Chicago Press, 1974).

7. Donald Schoen, *The Reflective Practitioner* (New York: Basic Books, 1983).

8. See, for example, Tom Peters, *Liberation Management* (New York: Knopf, 1992); and Tom Peters, *In Search of Excellence* (New York: HarperCollins, 1982).

9. Thomas A. Stewart, "Brainpower: How Intellectual Capital Is Becoming America's Most Important Asset," *Fortune,* June 1991, 44.

10. Ikujiro Nonaka, "The Knowledge-Creating Company," *Harvard Business Review,* November–December 1991; and Ikujiro Nonaka and Hirotaka Takeuchi, *The Knowledge-Creating Company: How Japanese Companies Create the Dynamics of Innovation* (New York: Oxford University Press, 1995).

11. Dorothy Leonard, *Wellsprings of Knowledge: Building and Sustaining the Sources of Innovation* (Boston: Harvard Business School Press, 1995).

12. Thomas H. Davenport and Laurence Prusak, *Working Knowledge: How Organizations Manage What They Know* (Boston: Harvard Business School Press, 1998).

13. BP's KM story is described in more detail in John Henderson and Lloyd Baird, *The Knowledge Engine* (San Francisco: Berret-Koehler, 2001). Also see Chris Collinson and Geoff Parcell, *Learning to Fly: Lessons from One of the World's Leading Knowledge Companies* (London: Capstone, 2001).

14. Stephen Denning, *The Springboard: How Storytelling Ignites Action in Knowledge-Era Organizations* (Medford, MA: Butterworth-Heinemann, 2001).

15. Len Ponzi and Michael Koenig, "Knowledge Management: Another Management Fad?" working paper (Brookville, NY: Long Island University Palmer School of Library and Information, 2002).

Chapter 9

1. Christopher A. Bartlett and Meg Glinska, "GE's Digital Revolution: Redefining the E in GE," Case 9-339-055 (Boston: Harvard Business School, 2002), 6.

Appendix A

1. Sources for the list include Catherine Hayden, *Handbook of Strategic Expertise* (New York: Free Press, 1986); Tim Hindle, *Guide to Management Ideas* (New York: Economist Books, 2000); Eileen Shapiro, *Fad Surfing in the Boardroom: Reclaiming the Courage to Manage in the Age of Instant Answers* (Cambridge, MA: Perseus, 1995); H. D. Stolovich and E. J. Keeps, eds., *Handbook of Human Performance Technology* (San Francisco: Jossey-Bass, 1992); and Richard Pascale, *Managing on the Edge: How the Smartest Companies Use Conflict to Stay Ahead* (London: Penguin Books, 1990).

INDEX

ABOUT THE AUTHORS

Thomas H. Davenport is the Director of the Accenture Institute for Strategic Change, a research center in Cambridge, Massachusetts. He is also President's Distinguished Professor of Information Technology and Management at Babson College. His previous books include *The Attention Economy: Understanding the New Currency of Business* (coauthored with John C. Beck), *Mission Critical: Realizing the Promise of Enterprise Systems,* and *Process Innovation: Reengineering Work through Information Technology.*

Laurence Prusak is a researcher and consultant who has taught in several leading universities on the topic of knowledge management. He is also a Distinguished Scholar at Babson College. Prusak is the author of *In Good Company: How Social Capital Makes Organizations Work* (with Donald J. Cohen) and *Managing Information Strategically* (with James McGee) and the editor of *Knowledge in Organizations.* He has also been published in several journals, including the *Sloan Management Review, Harvard Business Review,* and *California Management Review.*

Davenport and Prusak's previous books together include *Working Knowledge: How Organizations Manage What They Know* and *Information Ecology: Mastering the Information and Knowledge Environment.*

H. James Wilson is a writer and researcher at the Accenture Institute for Strategic Change.